How to Raise Courageous Kids

HOME GROWN HEROES

Tim Kimmel

MULTNOMAH
Portland, Oregon

Unless otherwise indicated, Scripture references are from the Holy Bible: New American Standard Bible, ©1960, 1962, 1963, 1968, 1971, 1973, 1975, 1977 by the Lockman Foundation. Used by permission.

Scripture references marked KJV are from the Holy Bible: Authorized King James Version.

Scripture references marked NIV are from the New International Version, ©1973, 1978, 1984, by the International Bible Society. Used by permission of Zondervan Bible Publishers.

Cover design by Multnomah Graphics
Cover illustration by Myles Pinkney
Cover photos by Butch Jannapolis

HOME-GROWN HEROES
© 1992 Tim Kimmel
Published by Multnomah Press
10209 SE Division Street
Portland, Oregon 97266

Multnomah Press is a ministry of
Multnomah School of the Bible
8435 NE Glisan Street
Portland, Oregon 97220

Printed in the United States of America.

Library of Congress Cataloging-in-Publication Data
    Kimmel, Tim.
    Home-grown heroes : how to raise courageous kids / Tim Kimmel.
    p.   cm.
    ISBN 0-88070-359-8
    1. Child rearing—United States. 2. Courage—United States. 3. Child rearing—Religious aspects—Christianity. I. Title.
HQ769.K488 1991
649'.1—dc20   91-41094
                                                                    CIP

92 93 94 95 96 97 98 99 00 01 - 10 9 8 7 6 5 4 3 2 1

Dedication

To Karis, Cody, Shiloh, and Colt:

heroes under construction.

Tim Kimmel conducts conferences on marriage and family throughout the United States. For more information about Tim's seminars, his availability as a speaker, or for his catalog of resources, write or call:

Tim Kimmel
Generation Ministries
P. O. Box 31031
Phoenix, Arizona 85046
(602) 948-2545

Other books by Tim Kimmel:

Little House on the Freeway: Help for the Hurried Home

Parenting with Purpose

Surviving Life in the Fast Lane: A Discussion Guide for Little House on the Freeway

Videos available from Tim Kimmel's Home Carpenter Shop:

"Building Confident Families"

"Building Close Families"

"Building Calm Families"

Contents

Acknowledgments

It's hard to write a book about courage without regular doses of encouragement. I'm indebted to a handful of people who believed enough in this project to continually voice their confidence in me.

Meredith Wheeler gave me free access to his guest room, his refrigerator, and his gifted mind. Thanks for keeping an eye on the forest while I was roaming among the trees.

John Trent, whose practical advice over a series of lunches would pass for the wisdom of the ages in anybody's book.

Mark Holmlund and Barry MacBan let me hide from my self-made distractions long enough to get this book from my heart to my word processor.

And my wife, Darcy. The distance between the starting blocks and the finish line would have been lonely were it not for the sound of your voice consistently cheering me on.

Foreword

America needs a new generation of heroes. We need men and women who don't wet their fingers and lift them to the air before they make a decision. We need people who are ruled by a conscience that doesn't take the Ten Commandments lightly—who have a fundamental reverence for their Creator, and a respect for the people and things He has created.

I've been kicking around the back roads and back streets of this world for three quarters of a century. I've enjoyed peace and I've endured war. But regardless of the times, one thing stands true: We live or die by our ability to produce heroes. Now we're inching our way closer and deeper into the next millennium. It's obvious the hope for our country lies in its ability to produce the kind of leadership that holds it to the principles that made it strong and the convictions that can keep it that way.

That's why I strongly believe our future depends on the integrity of parents. They are today's warriors fighting for tomorrow's victories by carefully grooming the boys and girls that will ultimately lead us. If you're a mom or dad, the question isn't *if* your boy or girl will have an impact, but *how* and *what kind?* To me you are our greatest asset.

I think you made a wise choice in picking up this book. It will give you confidence and freedom to do your part well. I've known Tim Kimmel for a long time, and I know how much his heart beats for the families of our nation. He's put together a set of principles that work. If you carefully apply them to your own life, you can turn them into grit and backbone in your kids' lives.

You'll probably never get a medal pinned on your chest or the recognition you deserve for all you have done, but your efforts won't go unrewarded. Your home-grown heroes will be medals of honor that you can wear with dignity. For your willingness to love your kids enough to build into their hearts the courage and resolve they so desperately need . . . I salute you.

Brig. Gen. Joe Foss (Retired)
Recipient of the Congressional Medal of Honor

Parenting
in No Man's Land

I adjusted the chin strap on my son's camouflage helmet and checked his ammunition clip to
make sure he had enough rounds for the coming
skirmish. Cody's combat boots were still muddy from
his last patrol. It didn't matter. We were going to war,
not a dress parade. We'd save the spit-n-polish for
the victory review on Sunday; right now I needed to
make sure his feet were protected. His flak jacket
was still new and too big for him. He'd grow into it
in time, but for now, it was better than nothing. If
the enemy thought for a second that he wasn't wearing it, they'd use his heart for target practice.

He was too preoccupied during my inspection

to concern himself with the threats that waited a mere two miles from where we stood. His eyes danced with anticipation; mine merely studied him with sober concern. Six years old is awfully young to have to make it through a combat zone, but we weren't given much of an option. The war was unavoidable—and we were committed to making it through alive.

We jumped in the car and headed for No Man's Land.

"Dad, can we park on the side of the mall where McDonald's is?"

"Sure, Cody." He had chosen a frontal assault, straight into the teeth of the enemy.

We weren't thirty steps inside the north entrance when we drew enemy fire. I saw it coming a split second before Cody but didn't have time to warn him. We were standing in the middle of a mine field with snipers trying to pick us off. Cody's flak jacket absorbed the full impact of the first shot at his soul.

"Dad, look."

"Yeah, Cody. What do you think?"

"I think that's a movie kids shouldn't see."

"I don't think that movie is good for anyone to see," I responded.

The advertisement for the slasher film was graphic and chilling—a typical fifty-ways-to-meet-your-Maker movie poster complete with blood, knives, and a disfigured killer with twelve-inch, stainless steel, press-on nails. Cody's flak jacket of faith did its job well. But no sooner had the sound of the gunshot died away than we set off a mine a few feet away.

Cody stepped right on it.

"Dad! Why is that lady taking off her clothes for that man? Are they married?"

The R in the lower right-hand corner of the movie poster virtually guaranteed that the provocative encounter between this couple had little to do with love, and a lot to do with lust.

"No, Cody. I doubt that they're married."

Cody thought out loud. "I don't think God would be happy with what they're doing."

"Right, son." His boots of the gospel of peace were helping him maintain solid footing. I just hoped he would stand as well ten years from now when the sexual temptations would be real life rather than air-brushed.

We spent an hour-and-a-half in the war zone that afternoon. My son's spiritual equipment protected him well. He needed the helmet of salvation in the T-shirt shop and the ammunition of God's Word while we ate our ice cream next to the Nintendo center. That's where the kids in the black heavy-metal outfits with the designs shaved on their heads were hanging out. They used about every profane word I'd ever heard in a conversation that lasted barely five minutes.

As we left the mall I thought of the battlefield Cody would enter Monday morning—one he had to face alone. My wife and I would continue to make sure that his battle equipment was adequate and in place, but our confidence in his safety would be challenged. So far, school had made him a better soldier, but we knew full well its reputation as a killing field.

Like it or not, I am the field commander of a small but significant platoon, and my son is one of four conscripts placed in the care of my wife and I.

We are to prepare them for the war raging against the moral security of the human spirit. Cody will need many skills if he is to prevail in battle, but all of them put together will fall short if he does not have the priceless quality called courage.

Today's parents have to lead with the future in mind—training their children to make it through the attacks of culture while keeping their souls intact. Like boot camp sergeants who prepare their platoons for every contingency, courageous parents groom their children to shoulder the future by leaning into the present.

As I walked with my son through one of the many war zones confronting a typical kid, I knew he would need the right offensive and defensive equipment. If he was to make it through, for the first few times he'd also have to be accompanied by a seasoned veteran. I knew that without courage, the battle would overwhelm him.

Sunday school theories only go so far when confronting real-life challenges. It's only when we put muscle behind our convictions that we see victory. That's why discussing faith without referring to courage is the best way to get creamed on the battlefield. Courage is the muscle that faith uses to hold its ground. Our theology is little more than rhetoric if it isn't lived out with resolve.

Take every hero of the Bible and you'll see the common link was courage. It moved their convictions from the heart to the head. It turned faith from an attitude to an action.

Some parents think the solution is to run from the battle or to keep their children as far from danger as possible. They avoid traps like the malls, put their kids in educational environments that don't challenge their convictions, and avoid as many contacts with the enemy as possible. That may *protect* a child, but their strategy falls short when it comes to *preparing* him. Unless you can raise your child in a hermetically sealed spiritual bubble, your child is going to need a potent ability to stand firm against the enemy. That's why twenty-first century parenting must include a careful plan for instilling courage in the hearts of our children.

Where Has All the Courage Gone?

The sad truth is that few kids today demonstrate courage. When I first started working with teenagers twenty years ago, I thought they suffered from a bad case of intimidation—an anemic belief system that made them easy prey for the forces of darkness. Two decades later I see wholesale cowardice, a nation's youth overwhelmed and defenseless.

The numbers don't lie. Teenage pregnancy, drug abuse, alcohol abuse, a cheating epidemic, domestic violence, and physical and emotional abuse crowd the columns of our newspapers and magazines. These kids' heroes are one-dimensional MTV icons or self-indulgent sports figures with "900" phone numbers. Let me tell you a few other things about this new generation of kids: they live at some of the finest addresses in the community and faithfully sit beside their parents in church Sunday after Sunday.

By the time they are sixteen years old they've learned more about the Lord, about the Christian life, and about the ethics expected of them than their parents knew after decades of adulthood. This new generation of overwhelmed young people is not suffering from a lack of knowledge. What's missing is an ability to courageously live out their faith.

Courage isn't a foregone conclusion of living in a Bible-believing family. It's the result of a curriculum that deliberately factors in courage with every spiritual/ethical training exercise. Courage isn't an accident. It's predetermined by those who wield the most influence in a young person's life.

It isn't that parents don't want to instill courage into their kids; it's just that they find the competition to influence their children's value systems so severe. They feel as if they're fighting a losing battle. Parents are attacked on many fronts and are so busy struggling for their own survival that they find themselves distracted from the job of preparing their children. Some have been attacked so often by their culture that they are shell-shocked. Let me mention just a few of the enemies taking the fight out of our families.

The New Fatigue

Parents today must contend with what I call "the new fatigue." It appears when mom and dad try to keep too many plates spinning in a world where the ground is constantly shifting.

Families are weary. The moral challenges are everywhere, from the clothes they put on to the food they choose for breakfast to the morning news program they listen to as they prepare to leave for work or school. Moral challenges croon from the car radio, peer down from the billboards, and wink at the office. And whatever the moral challenges may be for adults, they are intensified many-fold for our children. But they don't have the years of experience and the sophisticated emotional system to withstand them successfully.

Families are weary from over-scheduled days. We schedule ourselves with complex organizers, but they can't relieve our sense of being overwhelmed. Our organizers may help us remember all the things we have to do, but they won't *do* any of them.

Families are weary from the fatigue of uncertainty. Fickle economies, transient nuclear families, and overnight re-programming cause many parents to lie awake at night long after they should be in dreamland. We're too weary, too whipped. Our bodies might wake up each morning as we sweat away at our rowing machines, but our spirits ache for a long overdue rest.

Rapid Change

A second challenge especially points up the need for courage—high-speed change. Home FAX machines, jetting from Los Angeles to Sydney in four-and-a-half hours, a new map of Eastern Europe, the Pacific Rim, decline of labor unions, baby boomerangers, megachurches, Day-timers for preschoolers, biodegradable junk food, microchip children, cashless economies, information livelihoods, conglomerate "Mom and Pop" shops, 106 channel TV, maximum wage for minimum worth, remote control relatives, nanosecond parents, freeze-dried funerals, thirty-five-year-old adolescents, robotic reconciliations, and day scare centers—are you ready for tomorrow? Because, ready or not, here it comes.

The future is in our faces. It has prematurely arrived. And those who want to flee to a time when time could still be discussed in units of days, hours, and minutes are finding there is nowhere to hide. Trying to hole up at the end of the road in Nowhere, Idaho, doesn't work—it's got a satellite dish.

If facing the future calls for any attribute, it is courage. Too many are having to face too much, too fast. The speed and complexity of the future drives a stake into the heart of the family. Relationships run ragged, love is litigated, truth becomes tentative, and opinion grows omnipotent.

If we're going to prepare our children for the future, we're going to have to condition them to withstand constant and overwhelming change. Such a sophisticated ability to adapt will require down-deep-in-the-gut courage.

We need some home-grown heroes, courageous offspring raised in an environment that doesn't let change slap them around.

The Three-Barreled Howitzer

The new fatigue and rapid change alone would be enough to give us a run for our money. But I also hear something else—the rumble of enemy fire in the distance, the discordant tones of forces that desire the souls of our families on a platter. The Bible names three of them, and any one of them is enough to do us in.

The World. That infectious environment colors our values, assaults our character, and places question marks on God's moral exclamation points. It wants to keep us down by consistently tripping us up. I see this enemy peeking between the lines of my editorial page, resetting the ratings letters on the mall movie marquee, screaming from the speakers in my son's bus, and lecturing my daughter in her values class.

The Flesh. He peers at me in the mirror, he dances across my brain in quiet moments. When God says, "Why?" the flesh says, "Why not? Go ahead! Grab the gusto! Live for the moment." And he's so hard to defeat because he always has home-court advantage.

The Devil. More dangerous than ever, he fans the flames of desire. He hired an ad agency in the 1980s and a public relations firm in the 1990s. He looks so good, so charming, so clever, so in touch with our needs, so in line with the earth's agenda. But every time I see him, he's wearing a bib and having another family for dinner.

If we're going to survive the new fatigue, rapid change, and the salvos of this three-barreled Howitzer, we're going to need courage. And if we want our children to make it, we're going to have to pass the gift of courage on to them. We need families committed to becoming proving grounds for tomorrow's leaders, families who know how to supply basic training for future heroes.

Two Types of Heroes

It would probably help at this point if we clarify the kind of hero we're talking about. There are two types of heroes in the world, heroes by *default* and heroes by *design.*

Heroes by default are those men, women, and children who happen to be at the right place at the right time (or the wrong place at the wrong time) and are conscripted into an action that turns out to be highly sacrificial and beneficial.

Heroes by default make daily headlines in papers throughout the world. We applaud them for their willingness to get involved, to risk personal injury, and to place other people's needs above their own. Often we have public ceremonies with lots of speeches, citations, and plaques to honor these people. Everything they receive is well-deserved.

That's not who we're talking about in this book. Rather, it's the second category of heroes, heroes by design, who will consume our attention.

These heroes are men, women, moms, dads, grandfolks, children, or singles who daily make conscious decisions to respond courageously to life's dilemmas. They realize the chain reaction set off by each choice they make. They understand the laws of cause/effect and actions/consequences. For them, the challenges of life are pop quizzes for courage. Life to them isn't a sprint, it's an uphill marathon requiring an ongoing commitment to details, ideals, commitments, and convictions.

These people are rare.

They stand in great contrast to most who surround them. Heroes by design don't buy the myth that "standard operating procedure" means taking the path of least resistance. They accept chiding from friends who mock them for taking the long, painful, self-sacrificing path through the middle of all the challenges which press against their family. They consistently reject the "lottery syndrome" that has overtaken our culture—minimal risk for maximum reward.

Courage blows sweet and pure through the lives of these folks who are willing to rise above the spinelessness that marks our age. Deep in our weary hearts we all long for the tenacity needed to develop into a genuine giant of conviction.

That's what this book is all about. It's not written by someone who's had to spill his blood or lay
his future on the line. Courage has eluded me more
often than I care to admit. But, like you, I desire to
be more than someone taking up space and sucking
in air. I want to make a difference in the handful of
people who matter most to me. Four are especially
dear to my heart. They study me when I'm not looking and watch closely for cues and clues to life. You
have some little eyes watching you, too. Maybe that's
why you picked up this book. You want to make a
difference. You want to *be* a difference.

The good news is, it's yours and mine for the
taking. God has not reserved courage for the high
and mighty but for the rank and file. If we never rise
above "average" in our ability to parent our children,
and yet display courage—then look out future,
'cause there's going to be some powerful kids coming along behind us! You are the perfect candidate to
make the difference in your child's life.

Defining Our Terms

Before we look at several characteristics of
courage we need to pass on to our children, let's
make sure we clearly have defined what we're talking about. I find it hard to beat the clear, uncompro-
mised words that Webster uses to describe courage:

> Courage: mental or moral strength to ven-
> ture, persevere, and withstand danger, fear,
> or difficulty.

Courage isn't something we're born with. It's
something we acquire through a careful plan and
process. It's easier to pass on from our practice than

it is from our pulpit. If we want it in ourselves and want to give it to our children, we must understand what it requires. Courage is faith in action. It's convictions covered with sweat. It's other people's best interest becoming our greatest concern.

In the back bedrooms of your home are children who need a fighting chance at the future. You've been working overtime on their faith, you've committed yourself to their intellectual excellence, you've made a career out of studying their unique bents. You've been helping them discipline their bodies through sports and work. Now mix courage into the recipe and see what happens.

The pages that follow will show you how you can have what you so desperately desire to give. You'll study several truths about courage. They are the fundamentals that make it a reality. They're the very truths that can make your home a haven for home-grown heroes.

And it all starts with a little seed. . . .

The Seed of Courage
in Each of Us

When I received the call that Catie had died, I felt as if a little part of our family died, too. She wasn't our daughter, but we had sensed her presence at our dinner table for so many years that we couldn't help but feel her passing made our family circle smaller. That's how long we had been praying for her. Years. Every dinner. Regardless of which child asked God's blessing on the food, there was always a special request on Catie's behalf. She had become a fixture in our family.

Catie was the daughter of a gracious, unassuming couple who had been our friends for about a decade. We came to know Dan and Cay about the time Catie was born, back when their shoulders were soft and the crosses they carried were much lighter.

It was during her fourth year, on Halloween, when the doctors informed them that Catie had a problem.

Leukemia.

A four-year-old and Halloween were made for each other. Like any child, Catie had planned her costume for weeks. She had also imagined the sweet-tasting loot she would carry home from her visits to neighbors' houses. But *that* Halloween Catie dressed in her *Wonder Woman* outfit and trick-or-treated from a hospital bed. Her preschool mind never could have imagined the goblins that would haunt her throughout the evening. Between her fever, technicians drawing blood, a non-stop parade of medical staff in and out of her room and the whispers doctors exchanged with her parents, Catie found much reason for fear.

So began an ordeal that would take five years to complete, where hope would arrive and then turn around and leave—three times. That's how often she went into remission, and that's how often she fell out of it. On that third occasion, the doctors were painfully honest with her parents. No child on record had fallen out of remission three times and survived. Catie wouldn't change the statistics. It was five years to the day, on Halloween, that Catie's body finally gave out.

On that day, however, Catie did not lose, she only died. Her parents had prepared her for the moment. Because of it, she had been able to live her nine years on earth with confidence and grace.

Catie faced her ordeal with uncommon courage—not because of some extraordinary ability that overwhelmed her at the moment of death, but because of a carefully developed strategy her parents had laid out. Dan and Cay realized Catie would need courage to fight the cancer, and even if she lost the battle, she'd need it to face her death. That's what motivated them to set about the work of isolating the seed of courage God had placed within their daughter and then doing the things that would help it grow.

As a result, Catie was a home-grown hero. Groomed for bigger-than-big living by parents who understood a handful of fundamental truths about courage. The reason she was such an excellent example of courage is not for the way she faced her death, but for the way she faced her life. She didn't live like someone under a death sentence. She was an uncomplicated little girl who lived with enthusiasm, didn't begrudge God's sovereign freedom, and faced the inevitable with grace.

Her success came by design. That's what happens when you live in a home where courage is preached *and* practiced. It was so much a part of the fiber of the family that it would have been difficult for her to be anything but courageous. A courageous environment does that to a child.

Identifying the Seed

We need to recognize that God has placed a seed of courage in everyone. It's part of being made in His image. If we're going to build courage into our children, it's imperative that we begin with the assumption that this seed of courage exists.

The Bible assumes the seed is there. We see God addressing it as He speaks to the first offspring of Adam and Eve. I don't think Cain was born with a chip on his shoulder, but early on he picked one up. The biblical account makes it clear that a series of problems led to Cain's hatred toward both his younger brother Abel and God. God approached Cain with some advice. And in that advice we see God assuming the presence of a seed of courage.

> Why are you angry? And why has your countenance fallen? If you do well, will not your countenance be lifted up? And if you do not do well, sin is crouching at the door; and its desire is for you, *but you must master it* (Genesis 4:6-7, emphasis mine).

You must master it! God wouldn't expect us to master our inner urges if He didn't first give us the ability to do it. That's why it is probably not accurate to pray for courage. That's much like asking God for humility. The Bible says, "Humble yourselves, therefore, under God's mighty hand, that he may lift you up in due time" (1 Peter 5:6, NIV). It is not biblically accurate to ask God for humility, because His position in the Bible is, "That's not My responsibility, but yours." We start with the assumption that genuine humility is possible for us and then practice it out of obedience to God.

In the same way, He has placed courage deep within us. He wants us to cultivate it. That's why He said to Joshua, "Be strong and courageous." It was a command, not a request. God wouldn't expect Joshua to practice a quality He had not first placed within him. Once we exercise courage, God strengthens it. God creates opportunities to teach our children about this wonderful seed He has placed in their hearts.

Cultivating the Seed of Courage

Once we've accepted the existence of the seed, we need to do specific things to help it grow. But before we get to the specifics, let's remind ourselves of a few basics of horticulture. Growing seeds need soil, water, and sunlight. The seed of courage requires the same things.

The soil.

The soil where courage germinates and takes root is the home in which a child spends his early years. The first decade and a half play a huge role in establishing a strong root system that can withstand the pressures waiting outside.

Children are born with a long list of emotional needs which must be met if we want them to develop confidence:

• They need to belong, to have a firm confidence that they are part of a loving network of people who treasure them.

• They need to be recognized, to get our attention, to know their opinions are valued, their concerns are shared, and that we are truly interested in the things that interest them.

• They need to have a confidence that our love for them is not based upon their gifts, skills, or performance, but is unconditional.

• They need meaningful touch, a home where love is a hands-on commitment.

• They need to be valued, to be convinced in

their heart that "I must be very valuable to my father and mother—look how they rearranged their schedule because they'd rather be with me."

• They need to be good at something. We need to help them identify and isolate their unique and innate skills—and then encourage them to develop these raw abilities into lifelong strengths.

• They need to be affirmed as unique individuals; persons who can make a one-of-a-kind contribution.

It's in soil like this where the seed of courage either lives or dies. Of course, there is no perfect parent. None of us meet all these needs. But if we do even an above-average job, we give our children the foundation they need to move on to courageous living.

The water.

When the soil around a plant is parched, the roots cannot draw in nutrients. Water softens that dirt and permits the plant to feed. It also fills the plant with the moisture required to transfer the needed minerals to its various parts.

Rest is to children what water is to a plant. It is vital to the process of building courage into our kids. When children are given adequate time for reflection, relaxation, and rest, all the dimensions of their lives are strengthened. This principle was obvious during Operation Desert Storm, the U.S. military conflict with Iraq. Iraqi soldiers surrendered by the thousands. When questioned by Army interrogators as to why they gave up without a fight, they said, "We had lost our courage." After forty-seven days of constant shelling, little sleep, and inadequate conditions for rest, they simply ran out of resolve. Several significant battles in history were won after some of the worst retreats. The retreat allowed the army to regroup and refresh itself, and ultimately gave it the longed-for victory.

The sunlight.

When it comes to courage, the human heart needs to bask in the brightness of God's grace. When it does, it develops a tenacious attitude toward the things that really matter. That's why legalistic homes create spiritual cowards. Checklist Christianity doesn't offer the dynamic relationship with the Son of God that enables an individual to enjoy the magnificence of God's love. Grace should characterize our homes. When it does, we put ourselves in the best position to create home-grown heroes.

Weeding.

Boundaries and discipline are vital to cultivating seeds of courage. By keeping our children's garden free of the weeds that entangle their convictions, we give courage the option to grow deep and strong. Kids brought up in an environment of loving and patient correction are stronger kids. Their muscled emotions can endure the workouts an antagonistic world dishes out.

It's Never Too Late

Maybe you've felt kicked around throughout your life. You've never been the type to take a courageous position, either in the glaring issues or the daily grind. You wonder whether you have what it takes to be the kind of courageous parent who grooms courageous children. One theme that runs from the front of the Bible to the back is that as long as you're alive, it's never too late to do what is right.

When Howard Carter stuck his candle through a small hole in the ancient wall encasing the outer room of King Tut's grave, his eyes were unprepared for the dazzling wealth that had lain in state for over three thousand years. Like any archaeologist, he assumed the gold, silver, and hundreds of furnishings were the real treasure in this mummy's crypt. Yet there was another treasure, hardly detectable, yet invaluable. In drawered boxes and bowls near the sarcophagus of the young Pharaoh, Carter discovered grains of wheat that had been placed in the tomb to supply food for the king's trip through the netherworld. No one figured that seed which had lay dormant for over three millennia could ever sprout life.

But it did. Those seeds of wheat were planted, watered, and cultivated. And from those seeds came life. That wheat, which had sat in dark silence for so many centuries, proved to be the only thing alive in the whole tomb.

The seed of courage which God has placed in our hearts and in those of our children wants to take root and grow. It needs soil that is fertilized with truth, rich in the nutrients of love, and watered with rest. Once that seed of courage germinates, it can multiply in your kids.

Killer Courage

It was an annual event in our children's youth program at church. The pine derby races drew record numbers of participants as parents worked with their children to build the ultimate wooden racing machine.

I had helped my daughter, Karis, build her first one a couple of years earlier. It wasn't a bad attempt for the first try. In the intervening time we both learned a little more about what it took to win. Actually, the chances of winning the race were on the same par as winning at roulette. With over ninety participants, and some of the fathers being design engineers, we didn't believe we had much of a chance.

But there was another way we could win. They gave four trophies to the cars judged to have the most original designs. Here the odds were much more in our favor.

The second car I built with my daughter had the most original idea I'd ever heard. Karis had thought of it while I was building the car for my son Cody (his race was two weeks before Karis's).

"Daddy, what if we shaped it into a killer whale?"

"Like Shamu?"

"Yeah, Dad, we could paint it pitch black with a white underbelly."

The gears in my head were already churning as I tried to figure out how I would carve the five ounce piece of wood into the distinctive shape of the Sea World superstar.

A week before the race, Karis was playing with one of her girlfriends. Somehow, the subject of the pine derby race came up. Karis asked her friend if she and her father had built her car. The girl responded that they were finalizing their idea and he was going to build it that week. Her friend asked her if she had decided what to build.

"You bet! Dad and I are going to make a killer whale."

Her friend's eyes got big. "That's a super idea, Karis. I've never seen one of those at the race."

You know where this story's going. Karis and I built our killer whale while unbeknownst to us her friend asked her father to build the same thing for her. After ours was painted, we couldn't get over what a perfect replica it was of the whale we had watched in San Diego.

I was speaking in another part of the country that weekend but made sure my flight back to Phoenix would get me to Sky Harbor Airport in time to make the races. By the time I claimed my bags and my car, the race was already in progress. By the time I got to the church, they were awarding the trophies.

First on the agenda were the awards for most original design. I positioned myself in the crowd where I could see Karis. She was sitting next to her friend. I smiled and waved. She giggled and held up her car. I couldn't help noticing the car that her friend was holding. It looked like a clone of Karis's, with one exception—her friend's was better looking. It was smoother, shinier, and obviously painted with more skill. Her dad was a better craftsman than Karis's dad. I started thinking that the idea of a killer whale must have been more obvious than I had assumed.

They gave out fourth place, third, and second. Then the announcer said, "The first-place trophy goes to one of the most clever designs we have seen in a long time—a killer whale."

I was beaming at Karis and nodding my head in approval as she leaned forward in her seat in antici-pation of her name being called. She winked at me as an acknowledgment of the team effort we had in building it.

"And this year's first-prize trophy for original design goes to number . . ."

Karis, of course, didn't win. As she heard her friend's name called, confusion crossed her face. Disappointment followed an instant behind. Her friend raced up to the front to collect the trophy and then brought it back to her seat for Karis to admire. I watched from the crowd, unaware of anything else going on around me, except the deep hurt I knew Karis was feeling. She wore an appropriate smile, but I knew what she felt.

In a few minutes, the event was over and the kids were free to join their parents. Karis leaned into my chest as I gave her a hug of support.

"Daddy, I can't believe she'd do that. She had asked me a week ago what we were building. I never thought she'd steal the idea."

Part of me wanted to trivialize the whole event, explain that the outcome of these type of things are meaningless. But that would be avoiding the issue. The problem wasn't about cars or trophies or ideas. It was about friendship.

We talked about it for a moment and I realized that Karis wouldn't have any problem forgiving her friend. But she felt it would be difficult to trust her. This was a close friend she highly valued. She wanted to be able to restore confidence, but didn't believe it could happen automatically.

"Why don't you tell her how you feel?" My suggestion was one of those that are so much easier to say than to do.

"Daddy, I'm too afraid. What if she denies she did anything wrong? What if she rejects me?"

"Those are all possibilities, honey, but if you don't

honestly explain your feelings to her, you may find yourself harboring bitterness for a long time to come."

It was at this point that I reminded her about the wonderful gift God had built into her for occasions like this.

"Karis, it takes courage to be honest with friends, and God has given you enough courage on the inside to make it through this situation."

What I was doing for Karis is one of the essentials to making the seed of courage grow in our children's lives—we must help them see the seed is there. It was the same thing that Dan and Cay did when they realized that their daughter, Catie, was facing such a frightening future. They simply talked about courage with the assumption that it IS.

I listened from the other side of the car as she and her friend talked in the parking lot after church. I knew how difficult it is to be honest in times like these, but I also knew how bitterness likes to take root. And when it does, it chokes out any courage that we may have growing.

"You deserved to win the trophy because your Shamu was better than mine. But I never expected that there would be any competition for my design. You stole my idea. Friends shouldn't do that to each other. I trusted you and you let me down."

For the record, the friend never acknowledged that she did anything wrong, nor did she give Karis any assurances that it wouldn't happen again. But it didn't matter, ultimately. Because Karis shared her feelings honestly and without vindictiveness, she felt good about herself.

That night, I stopped by her room to kiss her good night. Her killer whale pine racer was sitting on the roll-top desk next to her bed. I picked it up and studied it for a moment.

"Karis, you know what I'm going to think every time I see this car?"

She shrugged.

"This car is going to remind me how courageous you are. In fact, your experience tonight might serve you a lot better than any trophy you might have won. You had the courage to confront, and the courage to forgive. As far as I'm concerned, you scored one of the great victories of your young life."

I did my best to water the seed of courage within her. And you know what? I think it's sprouting. I believe I saw a sprout stick its head up just a couple of days later when Karis's friend came over to our house. The happy giggling that filled the house was a dead giveaway.

Where Courage Starts

Isolating the seed of courage depends on us first verbally acknowledging its reality in our children's lives. From day one, we need to approach it as a presupposition rather than a possibility. This is more than a mind game—it's urgent if we want to see courage blossom in their lives.

How often do you mention the word *courage* around your kids? If your kids went into the Marine Corps, it would be part of the curriculum in basic training. If they were to become police officers or fire fighters, it would be part of their normal education. We can do the same thing. Courage can be part of our daily vocabulary.

It only makes sense. If we want courage to be part of our kids' lifestyles, we must speak of it consistently.

Just as we teach table manners or the disciplines of a musical instrument, we should talk to our children about living courageously. Remind them that it takes courage to make up with their siblings, it takes courage to shut off the television and get after their homework, it takes courage to maintain their focus on a specific goal.

We should remind them that courage is one of the qualities we are trying to build into them. It's easier for them to pursue a goal that is clearly articulated. When they know that courage is more than a plaque on the family room wall, that it is part of the family curriculum, they become more inclined to receive instruction.

But reminding our kids about the seed of courage within them is only half the battle. We must also *applaud* when that seed takes root. Courage is the heart of the word *encourage*, and there is no doubt courage increases with encouragement. Our eyes need to be keen and our ears sharp. We want to catch our kids taking a stand, pushing themselves to do something right when everything about them says not to. We need to notice when their actions result in courageous behavior. I've enjoyed it when my children come home from school and review an incident where they felt they had to be courageous. That means they understood that courage is a trait we want them to develop.

If we compliment our daughters for modest behavior, we enhance their chances of being courageous when their friends or the fashion designers want to dictate a more sensuous wardrobe. If we compliment our sons when they show respect and honor to their mother, sister, or a woman outside the family, it will make it easier for them to spurn locker room talk and take stands against friends who desire to ruin a girl's reputation.

When a dad looks his daughter or son in the eye and says, "You were right, regardless of the abuse you took, and I'm proud of your courage," we run the roots of courage down to new and stronger depths.

I received a letter the other day from a friend who had heard I was writing a book about courage. He wanted to encourage me in my work and also to tell me how much the priority of courage made a difference in his son's life. Dave writes:

> The other day my wife was doing some work back in my son's room. Jonathan, four, and Erica, four months, were in the room with her. She placed Erica on Jonathan's bed (near the wall) for safe keeping while she stepped to the dresser for a now-forgotten reason. In the couple of seconds and steps to the dresser, Erica rolled over several times and was poised on, and going over, the edge of the bed. My son, also on the bed, saw this and grabbed her leg as she was going over. My wife watched this in horror, but could not get back in time to catch the falling infant. Fortunately, my son held on with two hands until help arrived. My wife was both scared with this near miss, and elated with my son's performance.

> When I arrived home from work the event was over, but hearts were still pounding!

When my wife related all the facts to me, I declared my son a hero and smothered him with hugs and kisses. We celebrated with a meal at his favorite pizza place (you know, an animal band and more rides than a carnival) and rejoiced as a family. In fact, last night in a discussion we were having, he reminded me that he was Erica's hero and acted bravely to protect her. Some stories are worth retelling. I reassured him that he was my hero, too.

What little heroes are running around your house? Do they know they have champions in mom and dad who couldn't be prouder of the way their kids demonstrate courage? Like Dave wrote, "Some stories are worth retelling." Let's look for the stories that unfold under our own roofs.

Really, they're a lot better than fairy tales. These stories come true.

Courage:
The Natural Result
of Internal Disciplines

Jeff was a seventeen-year-old coward. He was afraid of sweat, intimidated by time clocks and deadlines, scared to fight his urges, and reluctant to admit that the network of loose ends in his life were of his own design.

He fidgeted on the couch, digging at something embedded in the fabric. Mainly, he was bored. But he was complying with his parents' wishes to see a counselor in return for access to the family car. I wasn't crazy about the arrangement, or the captive audience. But here we were.

"Tim, it's simple. I want freedom."

Like a skip in a record, Jeff kept repeating this

point. To his mother, his stepfather, his counselor at school, to me. Freedom.

"What do you mean by freedom?"

I had been through this conversation with lots of teenagers Jeff's age. For most, it was simply the normal movement from dependence to independence. It was healthy and necessary.

But Jeff was different. Born out of wedlock, emotionally and physically abused, he had not been given a secure foundation in his early years. Since then, his mother had become a Christian and his stepfather was committed to following Jesus, too. He was also deeply committed to Jeff. But it was the first time in this young man's life that yes meant yes and no meant no. Jeff was not responding well to the disciplines and standards of the stable, balanced home in which he now lived.

Books about people like Jeff were cluttering B. Dalton and Waldenbooks at our mall. The pop-psychological categories were "dysfunctional" and "emotionally co-dependent." Jeff also fell into a more foreboding category—"kids without conscience." He could look you straight in the eye and lie through his teeth. He was a thief, a pathological cheater, and manipulative. So far, everything had been petty enough to keep him out of jail. But a pattern had developed which, if it wasn't changed, would eventually turn the key in the lock. And on top of all of that, he was brilliant.

"To me, freedom means being able to do what I want to do, when I want to do it."

"And you're not free to do that now?"

"Are you crazy? Tim, I can't breathe without permission. I have to be up at a certain time, in at a certain time, and in bed at a certain time. School tells me what to learn, Mom tells me what to eat, and Dad tells me what to do."

"Are you sure it's freedom you want?"

"What do you mean?"

"Well, Jeff, you defined freedom as the ability to do what you want to do, when you want to do it. But you went on to list the constraints that you live under, like getting up, going to school, coming home, eating, and going to bed. By the way, does your mother really dictate what you eat?"

"Not so much everything I have to eat. But she bugs me if I eat junk or stuff that isn't real healthy for me."

"And that really ticks you off, huh, you know, not being encouraged to eat junk and being encouraged to eat healthy stuff?"

"Put that way, it doesn't sound so bad."

"No, Jeff, I suppose it doesn't. Moms tend to keep that up for your entire life so you might want to get used to that one. But let's go back to the other list, you know, getting up, school, coming home, going to bed. The thing that irritates you is that you have to do all of these things, and you don't really have any say in the matter."

"Right, Tim. That's exactly what I'm saying." (He seemed encouraged that this counselor was finally getting the message.)

"Well, I wonder, Jeff, if the real issue is not freedom, but confinement?"

"Say that again."

"It bothers you that you are confined, by time constraints, education constraints, diet constraints, rest constraints, and family constraints."

"Right!"

"And if your definition of freedom were to hold up, then you wouldn't have to submit to any of these constraints? Right?"

"Right! Right?"

"Well, I'm not sure, Jeff. Your definition of freedom sounds great, but I'm trying to pinpoint an example of someone who enjoys that kind of freedom. Can you give me one?"

Jeff named friends with nicknames like "Dead Meat" and "Cockroach," whose primary attributes seemed to be that their tattoos were spelled correctly. And they did seem to fit his description—with one exception. Their parents had abdicated their responsibilities and had long since left these boys to themselves. Which explained their alcohol problems and their time spent in the juvenile lockup. Since they proved to be poor examples, he moved to someone he felt certain would impress me.

"All right, all right, I've got an example of someone who is free."

He leaned forward with that look that said, "Come on, take a guess."

"I give up, Jeff. Who?"

"You!"

"Me? Tim Kimmel?"

"Yeah. You're free."

"Free to do what I want, when I want to do it?"

"Right, Tim. You call all the shots in your life."

I was thrilled to suddenly find this out.

"So you want to be free, *like me?*"

"Yeah."

"Humph." I brought my bottom lip over my top one and nodded. Then I got up and walked over to my briefcase to retrieve my checkbook. I returned and sat down next to Jeff on the couch.

"Okay, Jeff. Let's take a little peek at the freedom that I enjoy. Like . . . a . . . oh, how 'bout this one?"

I pointed to an entry in my check ledger.

"So? Arizona Public Service. So what?"

"Well, Jeff, I have to pay them a hefty sum every month. It all goes back to a cause-effect relationship between a switch on the wall and a light in the ceiling. My wife has gotten used to it. So have I. If I don't send the guys down at APS a check every month, they unplug my house."

I flipped another page.

"Speaking of house, Jeff, look at this one. That's Weyerhauser Mortgage. They're the people that let me call my house 'mine,' as long as I send them a check to this amount every month. No check, and they suddenly decide the house is theirs and tell me to get out."

I leaned over and grabbed a family picture.

"Cute family, huh Jeff? Well, these kids here picked up a habit when they were little called *eating*. They like it. They prefer opening the door of a stocked refrigerator. And they get testy when they go for the cupboard and find it empty.

"And while we're on the subject of testy, Jeff, Darcy here gets a little testy with me when I want to sleep in instead of helping get the family ready for the day. The people who pay me to come and speak to them get testy if I don't do my homework and keep up with what's going on. My kids get testy if I don't get home from the office by the time I told them I would. And I get a little testy if I can't get to bed by the time that my tired body dictates."

Jeff was half laughing, half angry.

"In other words," he said, "I'm never going to be free." It wasn't a question as much as a conclusion.

"Not the way you define it, no. But if you define freedom as the ability to do what you ought to do instead of the ability to do what you want to do, then I think you will be able to have all the freedom you want. You demonstrate the responsibility that goes with that kind of freedom, and I think your parents will get off of your case."

"It sounds to me like you're a slave."

From free to slave in one conversation! "Actually, I prefer the word 'servant,' but yes, Jeff, I'm fairly confined. And that's the point. Freedom is confinement. Everyone is confined, either by truth or consequences. That's what Jesus meant when He said, 'You will know the truth, and the truth will set you free.' Truth, by its very nature, has tight boundaries. Whether you like the truth or not is irrelevant. You can't do a thing about it. That's why it's called *truth*. And that's why submitting to truth sets you free. I'm free to enjoy the confinements God has built into life to set me free—confinements that protect me, make me responsible, and help me maintain good relationships within my home."

"You make it sound easy."

"For me, it is. It's the way I was brought up. But for you, it's a bit more complicated."

It was at this point that we discussed one of the foundational principles to courage: Courage is the natural result of internal disciplines.

Courage often masquerades as discipline. Jeff needed to see that confinements in life can be allies. The more he submitted to the responsibilities that go with love, the more sense of freedom he'd experience.

My conversation with Jeff is more than a year and a half old. The baggage he carries from childhood continues to weigh him down. But little by little, he is learning that small victories give way to big ones—that courageous living comes from daily, deliberate acts of resolve.

Choosing Courage

This chapter begins a series of principles designed to help us instill courage into our children. Each principle is essential and they aren't developed in order of importance. But at the same time, it is obvious that some naturally lead to others. The affect that internal disciplines have on creating courageous people is so overwhelming that I felt it had to be first. Without disciplines it's difficult to make any of the other principles a lifestyle.

When it comes to exercising personal courage, we usually wonder things like, "Will I have courage at the extraordinary moment to dive in front of a speeding car and push the kid out of the way?" Yet how many decisions like that will we face in a lifetime? Reality dictates that the lion's share of courageous living takes place in the daily grind, behind the lines, in the lonely places, among our allies, in our own hearts.

Since, then, the bulk of our battles are won or lost day to day, in the trenches, we need to be asking ourselves a question like, "Do I have the courage to face this monotonous moment with the same set of values and ethics I would bring to the highest challenge?" And taking it a step further, "Can I teach my children to do the same?"

We need to see the cause-and-effect relationship in all of this. Discipline develops common courage; common courage develops uncommon courage. Therefore, if we want children who display uncommon courage, we must raise them in an environment shaped by disciplines.

Courage works best when it is backed by a network of internal disciplines. Why? Because disciplined people do the things that other people don't want to do—but know they should. Let me give you an example.

We all know that debt is a coward's way to maintain the family finances. Twenty-first century financing says you don't have to wait, you can have it now. Credit debt has conditioned us to give in to our impulses. It takes a lot of discipline to stay out of debt and it takes a lot of courage to resist being reprogrammed by a credit card culture.

Disciplined people have learned one of the fundamental truths about life—*there are no short cuts.* Children who have spent years at the piano bench clapping out the rhythm, saying the names of the notes, and then carefully and repetitively playing their exercises know that excellence is a high-ticket item. Loving parents make sure that their children faithfully and carefully do their homework because they see that knowledge is only acquired with large investments of time, motivation, inspiration, and perspiration.

When our children know that the truly valuable things in life come with a price tag, they are less likely to succumb to a coward's solution. Debt is just one of the areas where you build their courage muscles. Love, romance, the work ethic, and the time commitments that go with maintaining friendships are easier to enjoy when developed from a disciplined platform.

Courage, Faith, and Disciplines

The relationship between disciplines and courage is developed in some of the earliest writings in Scripture. God had outlined His expectations for obedient living to His people. He followed these verses with promises of blessing for those who were willing to take Him seriously. But toward the end of the book of Deuteronomy, God mentions how courage must play a part, too.

> For this commandment which I command you today in not too difficult for you, nor is it out of reach. . . . But the word is very near you, in your mouth and in your heart, that you may observe it. See, I have set before you today life and prosperity, and death and adversity; in that I command you today to love the LORD your God, to walk in His ways and to keep His commandments and His statutes and His judgments, that you may live and multiply, and that the LORD your God may bless you in the land where you are entering to possess it. . . . So choose life in order that you may live, you and your descendants, by loving the LORD your God, by obeying His voice, and by holding fast to Him. . . . Be strong and courageous, do not be afraid or tremble at them, for the LORD your God is the one who goes with you. He will not fail you or forsake you (Deuteronomy 30:11,14-16,19,20, 31:6).

God spoke through Moses to His people, challenging them to a disciplined moral and spiritual life. But He knew there would come moments when Sunday school rhetoric would be out-shouted by the demands of a selfish and contaminated environment. That's when they needed courage.

If we want to pass along disciplined courage to our kids, there are a handful of principles we need to adopt.

1. Define your convictions.

Because courage exacts a heavy emotional price and requires overcoming a lot of adversity, it is impossible to make it a way of life if we don't have deeply embedded reasons to do so. Convictions are the muscles that maintain ongoing disciplines.

Determine the absolutes you want to live by. Without a moral compass, disciplines and courage are difficult to exercise and even tougher to maintain. One of the greatest gifts you can give your children is boundaries. Within the boundaries they're safe; outside the boundaries, they're insecure. Courage doesn't fluctuate along a continuum of one to ten. It either is or it isn't. And the only way your kids can know what courage requires is if they are driven by a highly defined, internal set of convictions.

Too many families today are trying to sail the turbulent seas of a contrary culture without any regard for the compass of God's truth. They applaud themselves as courageous for the way they face the challenges that confront them, not realizing that many of the challenges are a result of their own negligence. It's like straightening the deck chairs on the Titanic.

Many of us are too proud of our opinions to

yield to the timeless truths carved in the Sinai tablets. We stand with the majority and cling to our erroneous positions.

We need to keep in mind a simple principle about foolish positions: Even if fifty million people agree on a false assumption, it's still *false.* Our skills can take our families only so far. If we want to get them safely through the challenges that lie ahead, we need to be honest about where we are, know where we are going, and consistently develop disciplines based on clearly articulated convictions.

2. Model disciplines.

We all know it's easier to throw something than to catch it. Courage follows suit. We set a standard for our kids that will overshadow our teaching and out-shout our instructions. The disciplines we practice demonstrate our ongoing resolve to the better qualities of life. When our children see us live them out, discipline and courage kiss each other.

• It takes discipline to get up and go to work every morning, and it takes courage to do it when you don't feel like it.

• It takes discipline to not allow yourself to be programmed by Madison Avenue, and it takes courage to resist the appeal when the item you don't need is something you've always wanted.

• It takes discipline to maintain your weight, but it takes courage to face the biting morning air when it's time for your jog.

• It takes discipline to stay true to your vows, but it takes courage to stick with them when the difficult adjustments that come with all marriages beg you to reconsider.

• It takes discipline to resist compromise, but it takes courage to resist it when the compromise is something that would relieve an immediate discomfort (like cheating on a test for which you haven't prepared).

• It takes discipline to admit failure, but it takes courage to admit failure when the consequences are going to be extremely painful.

• It takes discipline to finish what you started, but it takes courage to finish when you've been knocked down and ridiculed throughout your efforts.

• It takes discipline to dream great dreams, but it takes courage to maintain those dreams when everyone around you is thinking you're crazy. (Thanks, Wright brothers!)

• It takes discipline to give your time to others, but it takes courage to give that time to people who don't seem to appreciate it.

Children will do what we do, regardless of how often we encourage them to ignore our actions and live by our advice.

A Family that Prays Together . . .

Internal convictions and modeled disciplines can help your children make courage a lifestyle. But there's one more thing we need to add to this list.

Prayer.

We need to pray for them to be courageous, out loud, in their hearing. When we put them to bed, when we pray for them around the meal table. We can bestow the blessing of courage upon our children through daily talks with God. When they hear from the lips of Mom and Dad a consistent request for God to strengthen their resolve, they'll know they have an ally in their home as well as in their heart. It will help them when they graduate from the corner bedroom to a fox-hole at the university. Life on the battlefield will come easier to them because their heroics were home-grown.

The bottom line is this: Disciplined lives produce courage which leads to God's blessing, while undisciplined lives produce cowardice which leads to God's judgment. You don't believe that? Then take a look at two boys named Hophni and Phinehas.

Profiles in Cowardice

You ought to read 1 Samuel 2:12-4:22. You need a feel for the people. You need to sense the pain, the frustration. But most of all, you need to study Eli.

High priest—a character profession.

Father—a character profession.

Eli held both positions. But he barely filled the job description in one and didn't come close in the other. The biblical assessment isn't hidden deep beneath the surface of the Hebrew text. It glares at us from the surface, leaving no doubt about the heart-wrenching results of a father who refuses to discipline his children. Listen, as the scriptures describe Eli's own flesh and blood. . . .

> Now the sons of Eli were worthless men;
> they did not know the LORD and the custom
> of the priests with the people (vv. 12-13).

Worthless.

Unbelievers.

An embarrassment to their father's name.

Let's give them the benefit of the doubt. After all, they were the preacher's kids. It's tough enough being a kid, but when you're a preacher's kid people grade you by a stricter and sometimes heartless scale. As difficult as that may be, however, that wasn't the problem.

Phinehas and Hophni, Eli's boys, didn't even try singing that song. Even if it were true, it would have made little difference. Their lives were the results of a father's errors of omission. They were the logical conclusion of a father backing down from his responsibilities.

Maybe the weight of the nation had been pressing too hard on Eli. Remember, he was the high priest. At this time in Israel's history, that meant he was the national conscience, the prime minister, head judge and the director of internal complaints. No one's going to question the fact that the man had some strong pressures distracting him from his responsibilities at home. But God's work isn't an excuse to turn our backs on our children. No man's work is, regardless of what he does or who he does it for.

Eli's work wasn't the reason his boys turned out the way they did. Eli was. He wouldn't discipline them.

Who isn't guilty of falling short in this category? That's why part of me wants to pity Eli. I know too painfully well how difficult it is to maintain standards and boundaries around children.

But the problem between Eli and his sons wasn't that he tried and failed, it was that he never truly tried. Love can cover foiled attempts, but it can't cover neutrality.

Eli's boys slipped through the foundational years without boundaries around their wants. They raced through their teenage years without bridles on their urges. By the time they were adults they were men driven without direction. Worthless. Unbelievers. Embarrassments.

As heirs to the priesthood, they used their access to the sacrificial ovens to rip off God and His people. Priests were allowed some of the burnt offerings for their own dinner table. But there was a way and a time. Hophni and Phinehas were concerned with neither. They grabbed the choice pieces of meat without regard for its giver or the God to Whom it was given.

But the greater blow to Eli's heart came when he learned of their escapades with the women who helped the priest at the door to the tent of meeting.

You can sense the heartache as we read of Eli's attempt at confrontation:

> Now Eli was very old; and he heard all that his sons were doing to all Israel, and how they lay with the women who served at the doorway of the tent of meeting. And he said to them, "Why do you do such things, the evil things that I hear from all these people? No, my sons; for the report is not good which I hear the LORD's people circulating. If one man sins against another, God will mediate for him; but if a man sins against the LORD, who can intercede for him?" But they would not listen to the voice of their father, for the LORD desired to put them to death (vv. 22-25).

Feeble, desperate, beaten down by shame and regret, Eli faces his boys. He's worried for them more than they ever would know. He knew two things that they chose to ignore. He knew that he loved them. And he knew that his love couldn't save them from the certain judgment awaiting them if they didn't change their ways.

I'm just guessing; the scriptures don't say. But I have a feeling Eli desperately loved his boys from day one. They lit up his day when they stopped by the temple. They made him melancholy and reflective when he saw how quickly they were growing up.

These weren't boys who failed to get loved. They just failed to get discipline.

My memory dusts off an old Sunday school lesson, Hebrews, chapter 12, verses 5 and 6:

> My son, do not regard lightly the discipline of the LORD, nor faint when you are reproved by Him; For those whom the LORD loves He disciplines, and He scourges every son whom he receives.

Does that mean you don't love a child if you aren't willing to discipline him? I don't think so. It's not, *if* you love them you discipline, but *since* you love them, you discipline them. It's a choice to place your love on the line in order to insure their future. It also says that God, the perfect Father, disciplines every son who comes to Him. That makes the point of this passage obvious. Every child needs loving discipline, and every parent who desires to love to the maximum makes the hard choices necessary for discipline.

So what held Eli back if it wasn't a lack of love? There had to be something, a reason why he would forsake such an obvious and crucial responsibility. I'll take an educated guess and bet the farm I'm right. It was either fear or laziness. It doesn't matter which because they are flip sides of the same coin. But they got to him. Big time.

I'm sure it was one of those two, because

they've tried to slip in the back door of my home, too. Just when I'm ready to take a stand for the best interests of my kids' character, fear steps in:

- What if you're too harsh?
- What if they reject you?
- What if you're wrong?
- What will people think of you?

Laziness works me over even more effectively:

- This is going to be a lot of work.
- This is going to tap emotional energy that you already spent at the office.
- They're just going to make the same mistake again.
- The effort isn't worth it.

Whatever and whichever, the refusal to discipline exacts its price. It did for Eli. And it did for his two boys.

Everything happened just as predicted. God was forced to do what Eli refused to. But by then, He had been pushed beyond discipline to judgment.

What a sad ending to an unnecessary nightmare. God's people removed God's ark from Shiloh. They treated it like a good-luck charm and thought that its presence on the battlefield might give them some advantage over the Philistines. This foolish mistake was encouraged by two men with no regard for the Ark or the God who dwelt between its two cherubim. In the process, Hophni and Phinehas were killed.

A messenger returned to Shiloh to tell Eli his sons were dead. The news threw him backward in his chair, his neck snapped, and immediately his broken heart beat its last.

It didn't have to end this way. But such is the cost of cowardice.

No one said discipline is easy. It's not. Discipline is tough. Doing it from a heart filled with love (which is the only way it is to be carried out) is harder still.

But harder and more painful than both is the certain pain we will thrust on our children if we fail to build their character and confidence courageously through regular and sensitive discipline.

Heroes are home-grown. Disciplined kids grow up to become courageous adults. Undisciplined kids grow up to become cowards—if they live that long.

The choice is yours.

Courage Assumes
an Apprenticeship

Let me grab *Webster's*. I want to read you something. Listen to this: "Apprentice: one who is learning by practical experience under skilled workers a trade, an art, or calling."

Now, think for a minute. Name a skill you *didn't* have to develop. Name anything people choose to do that doesn't require careful and repeated practice. In fact, lots of things people *don't* do require just as much practice. People who don't eat junk, who don't waste valuable time, who don't gossip, who don't pollute their mind, who don't defraud their soul—all of these people got that way because they practiced making good choices. Courage is no different.

Courage is an art.

Courage is a calling.

And courage is a skill. That's why there is another powerful truth we must embrace if we want to pass on courage to the next generation: Courage assumes an apprenticeship.

We don't use the term apprenticeship much anymore because we don't learn trades much anymore. Ours is an information economy and we tend to throw the concept of apprenticeship into a basement corner along with our obsolete tools and worn-down bars of pumice soap. But some things don't change, and character is one area that will always require an apprenticeship.

When we study *Webster's* definition, we see that a successful apprenticeship features at least three elements: a teacher, a learner, and a situation. Let's look at each and see how they apply to the creation of a courageous spirit.

The Teacher

The success of an apprenticeship has more to do with the teacher than the pupil. The reason is obvious. A pupil is restricted by the abilities of his teacher. That's why we waited in line at college. It wasn't so much the course as it was the professor who drew us to a particular subject. I can remember several courses in college and graduate school that I took, not because I had much interest in the subject, but because I wanted to log as much time as I could with a particular teacher.

Since so much of our children's success in life is determined by our effectiveness as teachers, let me suggest a checklist for a conscientious parent that might help in overseeing your child's apprenticeship in courage.

Know yourself and always seek improvement. Our lives are a tapestry of images, experiences, and memories that weave together into the person we reflect to those around us. Like it or not, we need to be honestly aware of what we are and what we aren't. If we fail in either of these two areas, my observation is that we are more apt to fail in understanding what we aren't. Let me list a couple of areas where parents fail to see themselves accurately and honestly.

• Some parents assume they're balanced when they're not. They are certain that their daily lives and internal attitudes are healthy and they therefore have an objective view of themselves and their family.

• Some parents assume they are sensitive, when they're not. This makes it difficult for them to gauge the speed and ability that their children can bring to the learning process.

• Some parents assume they are fair, when they're not. Kids are amazingly aware of preferential treatment, or the lack of it.

• Some parents assume their motives for having their children do or be certain things are because they genuinely want the best for their children, when their motives are, at best, tainted by their own insecurities and fragile needs.

Here's the problem. It's in the word *assume*. It implies that we know something. The problem with knowing something is that it tends to close us off to learning more.

If we're going to make assumptions regarding our qualifications for training our children, only one is safe. This is the assumption I try to bring to my own role as a father. I assume I tend to lack balance, lack sensitivity, fall short of consistent fairness, and operate with selfish motives. And assuming this forces me to my knees in dependence on God.

Most of us are, at best, a crippled substitute for the kind of teacher that our children's future requires. But in spite of that, God, in His sovereignty, has *chosen* us. And what's more, His truth can direct us, His grace can flow through us, and His work in our life can overwhelm our inadequacies.

Which brings up the second part of the suggestion: *Always seek improvement.* A surgeon who considers himself above learning anything new is going to kill somebody. A soldier who considers himself above learning anything new is going to kill himself. What distinguishes truly effective people is their insatiable appetite for improvement. They never assume they've figured it all out, and they keep themselves in a position where they can be evaluated. Make yourself vulnerable to people who can give you feedback—including the children you're trying to help.

The fact that you picked up this book is proof that you desire improvement.

Be proficient in the cultural struggles for the family. If we're trying to develop the internal muscle of courage in our kids, we need to be keenly aware of the challenges that face them. Courage assumes a battle. Its very existence is proof there are forces that need to be reckoned with. A military field commander is shrewd, and he or she maintains a constant inflow of information about the works, the ways, and the wisdom of the people or powers that seek to harm them.

Therefore, rejecting or ignoring the things that naturally draw kids' interest is tantamount to handing them over to the enemy.

For instance—music. It's normal for a parent to despise the music their teenagers find appealing. It's also fairly standard for parents to attack what they don't relate to when it comes to musical taste. Sometimes we take the easy way out (because it looks like we can defend it biblically) and simply forbid our children to listen to the music of their generation. The historical record has shown for centuries that this method of dealing with a dilemma doesn't work. But we consistently revert to it. Frankly, it's the lazy way, therefore, the coward's way to deal with the problem. Like it, or not, we need to lead from an intelligent position when it comes to helping our children make courageous choices in the area of music.

Music is just one area. Let me throw out a list of other people and forces that we need to be knowledgeable about if we are fulfilling our responsibility of protecting and preparing: their friends, their friends' parents, their friends' older brothers, their friends' mothers' live-in lovers, their textbooks, the movies they see, the television shows they consistently watch, state and federal legislation that bears on the family, the attitude of the community in which they live, their advisors at school or at sports, our jobs, and our employers' attitudes toward us as parents or spouses. These are just a few off the top of my head. And they are enough to keep us shuffling.

I mention these not to create guilt but to enlighten and inform. That's why, for instance, I like to read the Bible. It enlightens and informs me. It also makes me feel guilty. I see how far short I consistently fall. Whether I win or not is usually determined by whether I react or respond. I could ignore the message or slap the messenger, but in the end I only hurt myself.

Look for teachable moments. One of the more worn out sections of a parent's Bible ought to be the sixth chapter of Deuteronomy. I'm glad God had Moses put it there to remind us. It may keep us humble, but it also can keep us on target.

> Hear, O Israel! The LORD is our God, the LORD is one! And you shall love the LORD your God with all your heart and with all your soul and with all your might. And these words, which I am commanding you today, shall be on your heart; and you shall teach them diligently to your [children], and shall talk of them when you sit in your house and when you walk by the way and when you lie down and when you rise up (Deuteronomy 6:4-7).

Since each day is an opportunity for courageous living, each day should be a lesson. You get the feeling from this passage (and the verses that follow it) that God is saying to us, "Make my truth and my presence so much a part of each day that your children can't help but understand it."

Close the loop on your mistakes. It was December 27, Shiloh's fourth birthday. As usual, Darcy had fixed a hearty pancakes-and-eggs breakfast to mark the beginning of our celebration. Later on that day, several little girls would be over for her party, and then we'd cap it all off with some relatives coming by for dinner. So breakfast was like the gun at the beginning of the race.

I was in position with the video camera as Darcy approached the table carrying a stack of pancakes with four candles burning on top. We began singing *Happy Birthday to You*. We finished singing *Happy Birthday to You*. But one of our children didn't. This child knew some add-on phrases that had no relevance but sounded clever—to a child ("and channel four, and Scooby-doo, and . . ."). On and on and on it went. Meanwhile Shiloh waited to blow out her candles as melting wax mingled with melting butter. Then she began to panic while Dad groped for the shut off button on the camera so that I could vent my frustration.

"Enough! You're spoiling the celebration." I was ticked at how one child could draw so much attention from the star of breakfast to herself. So I made my feelings clear. I went into a lecture about poise. Poised people have a keen sense of the appropriate, and that it's not appropriate to upstage a person at her own party. My oldest daughter responded immediately and appropriately to my rebuke. She apologized to Shiloh and went to get some new candles. But I was still ticked. Something inside me wanted her to feel worse than she did. That quick apology had seemed too easy. So for another few minutes I reiterated what a mistake she had made.

In the process, I broke the very principle I was trying to teach. I must give a poised rebuke, and my overkill was inappropriate. I didn't see it at the time; it hit later that afternoon as I reflected on it at my office. *Why didn't you make your point, then leave it? Why did you have to keep pounding home the principle until it did more harm than good?* I didn't wait until I got home to close the loop. I picked up the phone.

"Let me speak to Karis. . . . Hi, honey. You know something? Sometimes Daddy puts in thumb-tacks with sledgehammers." She laughed at the thought even though she didn't know what it referred to. I went on to explain how I had broken the very principle I had been trying to teach by the way I had reprimanded her at breakfast. "Now it's my turn to apologize. . . ."

If we leave a series of loose ends in our rela-tionships with our children, they're going to have difficulty appreciating or absorbing the truth we are trying to transfer. Effective apprenticeships some-times require a healthy slice of humble pie. Take it from someone who could write a recipe book on the subject.

The Learner

Know your family members. Just as there are myriad forces pressing on our family from the outside, there are myriad forces pressing from the inside of each of our children. And there is a different set in each kid. My wife and I have four children. We marvel how four children, who resemble each other so much, could be so different. We talk to their teachers, Sunday school teachers, coaches, friends, and their friends' parents to learn as much as we can about their uniquenesses. That way we can tailor our instructions to the things that make them who they are.

Our third child is a winsome little blond named Shiloh. When it comes to being a student of your chil-dren, this girl is not an easy read. She's complicated.

And even though she brings day after day of delight to our home, the more I get to know her, the more I realize she has been given an extremely sophisticated set of emotions. All of our children have fragile emotions (all of yours do, too), but this little girl requires a greater degree of understanding. She has been one of my greatest motivations for daily prayer as I come before the Lord for wisdom in being the father she needs.

Employ your family members according to their uniquenesses. Too many parents assume their children all have the same interests and abilities they have. We might be gregarious, friendly, aggressive, and naturally determined. Our son might be quiet, reflective, reserved, cautious. We need to adapt our instruction to their uniqueness.

One of the most damaging things a parent can do to a child is to foist unreasonable expectations upon them which are solely designed to feed our own ego. You don't train an effective apprentice by requiring him or her to do that which is beyond their ability, temperament, or skill level. And yet that is precisely what some parents do.

I wasn't there when this happened, and it's probably best I wasn't. The scene was classic. A little league game. Bottom of the sixth. The tying run on second. The winning run at the plate. Two outs.

The boy was too scared to swallow. This was more responsibility than he was ready for. He could barely see the balls that were burning by him. But with each one, the outlook got worse. "Strike two."

He put a choke hold on the bat. His jaw set. His teeth nearly crushed each other. The wind up. The pitch. He wasn't going to let this one get by! With all of his might, with all of his spirit, he swung . . .

But it wasn't enough. "Strike three!"

His head dropped, his eyes glazed. He turned toward his teammates who were already starting to gather their gloves and gear to head home from their defeat.

This is when a boy needs a parent's loving arms slipping around him and an encouraging whisper that reminds him he'll nail it next time. But that's not what this boy got.

The father's ego was wrapped up in his boy's performance. The rage in his father's voice boomed above the crowd. He shouted his disappointment with his boy in words that sailors shouldn't repeat. Then he did something that left a sick taste in witnesses' mouths for the rest of the day.

He made his boy strip down to his underwear in front of all the people, screaming at him that he was not worthy to wear the uniform.

The boy's humiliation was complete—for the rest of his life.

I wish I had been there, but it's best that I wasn't. My inclinations would not be honorable. I'd want to reach a finger through the chain link backstop and grab that father by the face, then ask him a question. "Do you remember the day that you were born?"

"No."

"Well, I'm going to reenact it." Then I'd pull his body through one of those little holes in the fence.

I wonder what we're thinking when we place on our kids expectations primarily meant to meet the voids within us? But we do. You don't build an effective apprentice that way.

The Situation

Create opportunities for them to learn or practice courage. I call these "planned dilemmas" and I pray for them to come into my children's lives every day. That probably sounds cruel, but if you understand my thinking, you'll see the practicality of it.

I pray for my kids on the last half mile of my morning jog. I ask the Lord to give them some dilemma at school or with their friends where they will be forced to make courageous choices. I ask this right after I've asked God to protect them from the people and powers they are incapable of standing up to. No parent wants the negative forces to work over their kids. At the same time, we know that muscles that never have to flex won't be ready when solid challenges come up. I like to pray that they'll have the courage to stand up for the truth, reach out to the rejected, refuse to participate in humor or rumor that is at someone else's expense. And it's interesting to see how God faithfully answers these requests. Sometimes the kids struggle. But every time they succeed, they increase their propensity toward courage, they see it for what it is—one of the greatest attributes in the divine treasure chest.

One of the best ways for them to understand courage is when you demonstrate it. Take them with you when you are going to talk to someone about a problem or conflict. A dear friend was concerned about the new NC-17 rating on movies in the mall. This was a way that film producers could get films that would otherwise have had X-ratings (and therefore banned from shopping mall theaters) into the conglomerate theaters. My friend was concerned about those kind of films being screened right next to a G-rated Disney film. There were numerous and logical reasons why this was not in the best interest of the community.

He went to the theater manager twice to discuss the matter with him. And each time, he took his daughter. She prayed with him in the car before they went into the theater. She saw how her father intelligently and graciously logged his concern. She saw how her father showed kindness to the theater manager even while disagreeing with him. She also saw the affect that her father's sensitive courage had on softening the theater manager. Ultimately, their visit affected the manager's attitude, and he put actions in motion that helped convince the theater owners that it was not in the best interest of their customers (and therefore, the theater's bottom line) to be showing such films in a mall venue.

Remember, We're The High-Water Mark

I hope these suggestions help, but we need to keep in mind that they are only as effective as we are. Without a courageous example from us, our teaching is useless.

We need to model a courageous spirit in such a way that our children pick it up simply through their daily contact with us. If we grasp this simple fact, we are already halfway to our goal.

We can pray for courage, but I'm not certain God is going to overwhelm us with it. Courage—like faith, integrity, obedience, and endurance—is not so much something God gives as it is something He blesses. And it is in His blessing that we watch these qualities multiply within us. He told Joshua, "Be strong and courageous" and every time Joshua courageously stepped out, God strengthened his resolve. So much so that he finally confronted the people of Israel at the end of his leadership and said,

> Make up your minds. You can follow the heathen gods of your foolish parents or the heathen gods among the foolish Canaanites. But as for me, and my family, we're serving the Lord (Joshua 24:15, author's paraphrase).

He had followed the courageous path so much that it became the habit of his entire family.

That's what we long for. You and me. We need it, like we need Jesus, every minute of every day.

We Are the Journeymen

We dads come home from a rugged day at the salt mines. Emotions have been spent, energy long since gone. Our minds have been picturing the couch and what it will feel like to sprawl out and vegetate for an hour. We reach up and pinch the button on the garage door opener. As the mouth of the garage lifts open, little legs appear at the base like teeth ready to devour us. They're there. Waiting.

"Dad, can you help me on my piano lessons?"

"Dad, can we play catch now?"

"Dad, will you help me with my geometry?"

"Dad, can you help me change the oil in my car?"

There's a family saturated with individual needs pleading to a father whipped from work. We have an option. We can go into a tirade about how hard we worked, how tough a day it's been, how much we need rest. The words fall flat on each one. Your wife has barely arrived home from her own wrestling match at the office, or she has been sweating it out in the equally overwhelming salt mines of the home. She's not going to be very sympathetic.

The kids can't understand—because they're kids.

We want Brokaw. We want quiet. And we can even justify our wants. But our wants have come up against our families needs, and fatigue wants to determine who wins.

That moment requires courage. Suck-it-up-and-face-the-music courage.

On and on it goes. It's called the courageous lifestyle. It's a choice. When we make that choice we touch eternal chords. We activate the powers of heaven to surround us with strength.

And little by little, that strength grows into a force that infects the very people we love the most.

Home-grown heroes. They are a byproduct of courageous parents. They are cultivated daily through the careful actions of faithful journeymen. And we can watch them grow by letting our children . . .

    watch us forgive
    watch us laugh
    watch us fight fair
    watch us make up
    watch us listen
    watch us teach
    watch us learn
    watch us proudly lose
    watch us humbly win
    watch us pray
    watch us hope
    watch us cry
    watch us praise
    watch us suffer

watch us prevail
watch us live—and ultimately,
watch us die.

In a good apprenticeship, all these elements come together. Of course, they don't come together easily. Apprenticeships take a lot of effort on both sides, apprentice and journeyman alike. And sometimes the toughest lessons aren't earmarked for the apprentice.

Who Would Know?

Paul was working late. Actually it was only 4:00 P.M. Normally he would still have an hour and a half left before quitting time. But today was Christmas Eve, and as was the tradition of his company, everyone had worked until noon, had the annual Christmas party, and then closed the office at 2:00. It was a gift from the guys upstairs. Normally at five minutes after two "not a creature would be stirring." Employees would be on their way for some last-minute shopping at the mall—a few errands before joining the family to celebrate.

But the company had received a pile of orders in the mail that day. That meant there were thousands of dollars worth of money orders and checks that needed to be posted. Paul figured it would be better this way. If he processed the orders now, he wouldn't have a mountain of work facing him when he came back to work the day after Christmas. Besides, he had no errands to run or last-minute shopping to do, because both would require money. And he had no money. He had already prepared his kids for the reality. It was going to be a bleak Christmas.

Normally the tree would be surrounded by piles

of presents. But normal Christmases require a normal year leading up to it, and it had been anything but a normal year. His wife had undergone surgery, then complications set in. His station wagon lost its transmission. His oldest daughter was fitted for braces and his youngest was fitted with temporary teeth to replace the ones she lost when she took a foul ball at the Pirates' game. The roof finally demanded replacement, and a third of the pecan tree smashed the storage shed during a July thunderstorm. He had insurance, but it didn't cover everything. He made a decent salary if nothing unforeseen happened and there was no such thing as inflation. But a family of six is a parade of unforeseen events, and for the past ten months the national economy had been in a bad mood.

It had been a merciless year.

Christmas carols played from a radio at the other end of the office. It was a lonely serenade as Paul pored over the envelopes on his desk. The money orders and checks ranged from $250 to $500. There were more than fifty of them. *They're going to be busy next week*, he thought about the guys in shipping.

His letter opener slit open another envelope and his fingers moved involuntarily to separate the order form from the money order. But this time he felt the distinct texture of cash. Four, fresh $100 bills. He fanned them in his hand to count them again.

They rarely got cash in the mail, mainly because they sold high-ticket items. Few people were willing to risk large sums. The reasons were obvious. And the scenario Paul found himself in was exactly why you weren't supposed to send cash.

Fact: No one was looking over his shoulder.

Fact: He could dispose of the order form and claim it was never received. Fact: He wasn't the only one that processed the orders. If an investigation followed, it would have to scrutinize four other people. Fact: That $400 could buy all of the gifts his kids wanted and still leave him enough to buy a decent bottle of perfume for his wife and replace her worn-out robe. Fact: The stores were open until 6:00. He still had enough time.

But his soul leaned those thoughts against the backdrop of a lifetime of integrity. Because he had apprenticed under his parents in the school of honesty and had continued his lessons as an adult, he made the courageous and moral choice to endure an affordable Christmas rather than enjoy a counterfeit one.

That $400 spent the Christmas holiday locked in the company safe along with the rest of the money orders. That night, Paul slept with a clean conscience and arose the next morning to exchange homemade gifts with his children.

The greatest gift he gave them, however, wasn't wrapped in bright paper or bound with ribbons. It was clothed in old pajamas and thatched with graying hair. It was his consistent habit of integrity, a journeyman's regular practice that would give his young apprentices the best chance of finding courage when facing their own temptations in the future.

Effective journeymen are like that. They are living proof of what Jesus said in Luke 6:40b— "Everyone who is fully trained will be like his teacher (NIV)."

Such journeymen have the remarkable habit of training apprentices who turn out just like themselves.

Courage Operates Outside Areas of Strength

R-I-S-K. For Jeannie it was the queen-mother of dirty words. She wasn't wired for it. It was something for the stout and hearty, not a part of the cushioned life she lived. Okay, maybe her life was routine, maybe she was routine. So what? It was what her temperament demanded. She despised venturing into the unknown.

But at that moment, hanging in the rappelling harness off of the eastern cliffs of Elevenmile Canyon, she was up to her teeth in risk. *What had she been thinking?* She had seen the ad for the Wilderness Club in an outdoors magazine. The breathtaking pictures of the rugged Rockies appealed to her esthetic nature. Since no other options had surfaced for a summer vacation, she figured photographing the Rocky Mountains for a week would be as good a diversion as any.

What the ad had failed to communicate were the demands that would be made on her energy and spirit to get all of those "Kodak opportunities." And nothing could have prepared her for the terror that would paralyze her while standing at the top of a cliff watching a fellow rappeller adjust the rope through her carabiner.

"Nothing to worry about, Jeannie. Just belay off the side once you're ready. We'll have you secure at both ends. And, Todd, down there at the bottom, he's the best in the business." He laughed. "Enjoy your fall."

It wasn't funny! "Fall." "Risk." The four-letter words were working her over. It took fifteen minutes of preaching from her instructors to get her to lean her weight into the harness and let herself drop over the edge. Her body went limp, bumping against the granite cliff before her. With tears tumbling to the ground eighty feet below, she wondered why something so simple for others was so impossible for her.

———

Arlene dangled from the precipice of life, tethered by tubes and wires that monitored the faint spurts and sputters of her fading, fleeting life.

Jeannie rested her forehead on Arlene's hand and buried her face into the hospital bed. Tears bathed her sweet friend's hand as she whispered to the God of Mercy to do whatever He was going to do—soon.

Cancer would claim another victim, probably before the night was over. Jeannie wanted to spend as much time as was left comforting her friend before she released her for her walk through the valley of the shadow.

For Arlene, it was just the shadow. Because of what the God-Man accomplished on a cross some two thousand years before, Arlene had only to concern herself with a mere shadow. Her soul was in the safe keeping of the Savior from Galilee and she was anxious to rest her beaten body on His chest.

Jeannie prayed. Tender, quiet words that touched a dying girl and gave her courage for the journey. Jeannie cried, weeping for Arlene's mother who sat helplessly watching her pride and joy slip from her fingertips. And Jeannie sang—low, faint words of praise to the God who gives and takes away.

Jeannie stared, without flinching, at approaching death. Tubes, syringes, dripping IVs, and catheters never dampened her resolve to stick by the side of a friend she had loved for so long. Arlene's chokes drew Jeannie closer, her withered shell unable to repulse or repel. Jeannie was at ease with sympathy, giving mercy to a friend at the end of her rope.

At 5:05 A.M., Arlene went Home. Jeannie thanked God for the rest and joy and beauty her friend was now experiencing.

Two scenes, same woman. In one, Jeannie was Jell-O, in the other she's a rock. The chances of her losing anything on her rappelling expedition were almost nil. The chances of her losing something on her visit to Arlene were 100 percent. She stood at the top of Elevenmile Canyon with the finest ropes, harnesses, carabiners, and instructors that a rappeller could want—still she was terrified. She sat at the side of Arlene, who had no chance, even with the finest equipment and technicians available on earth—and she was brimming with confidence.

Why? What makes the difference?

The answer has a lot to do with how much we will enjoy a courageous lifestyle and how effectively we can pass it on to our children.

Strengths and Weaknesses

Jeannie was strong through her bedside vigil with her friend Arlene because she was naturally gifted in that area. She had developed her gift of mercy so much that it wasn't difficult to meet her friend's need. Oh, it was painful. It was sad. But the shadow of death did not intimidate her because she was internally wired to be strong when in the presence of someone with great physical and emotional needs.

Elevenmile Canyon was another story. It showed up her weakness. That's why it had the best of her even before she slipped off the side.

Everyone has strengths and weaknesses. The strengths make us valuable to others, the weaknesses make us dependent on others. Both are necessary to human love. Love can't be enjoyed if it isn't both given and needed.

I'd like to look for a moment at this matter of weaknesses in our children's lives . . . even though by doing so I am taking a risk.

Weaknesses

Do you know what the risk is? It's that we'll do more of what we already do too much of. It's unfortunate, but most parents (including this one) have a tendency to overemphasize the weaknesses of their children. It's a combination of our kids' strengths being unrefined and their weaknesses consistently popping up at the wrong time. Regardless, building home-grown heroes requires us to help our children come to grips with their weaknesses. Let me suggest three ways.

1. Help them identify their natural weaknesses.

Usually weaknesses can prophecy what a strength will be. For instance, you may list as a weaknesses that your daughter is chronically late. That could indicate a few good things about her. Maybe she is very friendly and she spends so much time getting close to people that she loses track of time. Unfortunately, what she gives to one, she may rob from another. Weaknesses are often strengths pushed to an extreme.

Some weaknesses, of course, are the result of immaturity, sin, or a frustration from the past. We all have some of these and we need to work on them accordingly. But weaknesses that are strengths pushed to extreme can become areas where we can exercise courage.

2. Help them face their weaknesses.

It's difficult for some people to acknowledge personal weaknesses. Pride and insecurity push them to deny what is apparent to everyone else. Some parents have trouble acknowledging weaknesses in their children. They take it personally. Especially if it's in an area where those parents desired proficiency in their child. An athletic father might have a hard time accepting that his son has no natural coordination and athletic timing. Without an honest assessment of our children's weaknesses, we may be bending them in the wrong direction. It's a sure way to snap their spirits.

On the other hand, there are some positive things about weaknesses that can help our children make the most of them.

First, we need to help them see that their built-in inadequacies were put there by God for good reason. One is so they would be forced to lean on Him. We weren't designed to be self-sufficient, but God-sufficient. A second reason is so that they would be forced to need other people. We weren't meant to sing a solo through life, but to chime in with the choir. A third good reason for having weaknesses is so that we can learn the internal qualities needed for exciting living. We learn both trust and courage when we face our weaknesses.

We must also stress that weaknesses don't mean our children can't do something; it merely means it won't come easy. They have to apply more sweat. Beethoven was deaf. Thomas Edison was written off as a scholastic misfit. The key ingredients in their ultimate successes were parents who taught them to overcome their inadequacies.

Like it or not, our children won't get the luxury of functioning exclusively in the areas where they are strong. Although they will never be all things to all people, they must be willing to stretch themselves for the sake of other people's needs.

Your daughter might be shy, but there are times when she must be bold. Natural leaders have to learn to follow. Aggressive people must practice gentleness. The outspoken need to be vulnerable to others' critique. The methodical must be willing to be spontaneous. The moody have to be courageous enough to take responsibility for how their mood swings affect others. Stoic personalities need to learn that God gave them tear ducts just like everybody else. The self-sufficient must place themselves in predicaments that might leave them vulnerable.

It is especially when we step outside our areas of strength that we are forced to exercise faith. That takes courage.

When our children accept their weaknesses, they're in the best position to turn those weaknesses into assets. They're also in position to develop enormous courage.

3. Help them make a plan to courageously function in areas of weakness.

I have a close friend named Kory. He's a conscientious father, a careful steward of the children God has placed in his life. His oldest son, Seth, is a physical clone of his father. His father is 6'4". Seth is in ninth grade and can already look his dad in the eye. Kory was an All-American safety on a Pac-10 football dynasty. But his athletic ability was a result of taking above average size, average ability, and stirring in gallons of sweat. Seth has done the same. I don't doubt he will be all-conference in basketball. He can already give his dad a run for his money on the court.

Kory was telling me about something he

noticed in his son. Seth is not only similar to him physically, he is a carbon copy emotionally. He's quiet. Reserved. He doesn't initiate friendships, but responds well to the efforts of others. I didn't doubt Kory's assessment of his son, but I found it difficult to believe Seth's personality was remotely close to Kory's. Kory is quiet, but he seemed anything but reserved when it came to relationships. That's when he filled in a gap in my knowledge of his life.

By the time Kory graduated from college he had become keenly aware that he lacked certain natural people skills. He was an intuitive thinker, a problem solver, and an organizer. People posed too many abstracts for his tastes. But he knew that if he wanted to function properly among people, he needed to develop certain abilities that weren't naturally his. That's what led him to take a sales job after graduation. He had to "cold call" clients for a large Phoenix firm. He owns his own business now, and it involves a lot of calling on customers. Because he worked hard at an area of personal weakness, he can now call on strangers without difficulty. It still doesn't come naturally, but his courageous commitment to mastering an area of weakness has turned that weakness into an asset.

Now that Seth is heading for high school, Kory has helped him develop a plan that will enable him to flourish in relationships even though he is not naturally gifted in that area. His strategy will help Seth meet different people from the various social strata of the typical high school. He's also showing him how to move these people from acquaintances to friends.

I don't doubt that quiet Seth will have little difficulty turning his weakness into an asset. His father has already demonstrated it can be done.

Help Them on Their Way

It takes a lot of courage to face weaknesses. But it's a lot easier if someone is willing to go with you through the pain and frustration that often accompanies the process. It is even more encouraging when the person walking you through the weakness is just as vulnerable as you are. In order to build courageous kids, we may have to accompany them through areas that intimidate us, too. But when we do, we help their spirits soar.

Let me illustrate this principle, and close off this chapter, by pulling a painful file out of my own life. It was one of the great lessons I learned about courageously facing my own weaknesses. And I don't think I could have done it were it not for a friend who was willing to walk with me through it.

I remember it as if it happened yesterday. Darcy's smile was painted on. It was so convincing that I would never have thought she could be harboring such sad news. But I married a classy woman with a shrewd sense of timing. And in her sophisticated way, she knew the "welcome home" celebration took priority over the news of the home-going.

Four days of pretending to be a deer hunter had come to an end. My fellow hunters were milling around in front of our house as I unloaded camouflage gear, sleeping bag, and an unfired rifle. Hunter's hyperboles were flying back and forth as Darcy learned about all the deer that got away.

Finally, the noise turned to quiet, the confusion to calm. As my friend's Suburban pulled away from the house my mind was already in the shower, and as quickly as possible I wanted to put me in there with it. The only thing better than leaving on a hunting trip is getting home from one. I was anxious to wash off the woods.

Darcy took my hand and pulled me back out to the front of the house. She wanted to get me out of range of little ears that hadn't yet heard the news.

"Tim, your mom died last night."

It's remarkable how few words it takes to completely alter the way you view yourself and your future. Others have had to face life-changing dilemmas with only one-sentence warnings:

"We're sorry, but we did everything that we could do."

"You're fired."

"I want a divorce."

"You've been declined."

"Your daughter has leukemia."

We all get our turn at having reality pounded into our hearts with these single-sentence sledgehammers. But nothing prepares us for their bluntness or their numbing pain.

"Mom's gone, huh?"

Darcy nodded and started to cry. Like a knot that finally got untied, her hurt poured through her eyes. I held her as she whimpered on my shoulder—and absorbed her tears for Mom, for herself, and for me.

In the hours immediately following Darcy's announcement, I found myself wondering more about me than Mom. A guilt slowly built inside of me that I couldn't figure out. It wasn't a guilt about my relationship with Mom. She had maintained a "no regrets" status with everyone in her life. Everything was fine between us. But something was clearly missing as I pondered my loss.

It took me until late that evening to put my finger on it. But once I did, I recoiled from the thought.

I was sickened to see that within five minutes after Darcy had broken the news, my emotions had shifted into neutral. I felt nothing. I should be teary eyed, but there were no emotions to start the flow. I should be thinking of all the good times I had growing up with Mom, but I couldn't conjure any. I should be talking about her, reminiscing to Darcy and Karis, but I didn't breath a word about her. It was as though I heard the news, thought about it for a few minutes, then acted like that segment of my life never happened.

I was grappling with a part of my psychological makeup that had haunted me since childhood. It wasn't that I was incapable of crying, but I had always found it difficult to allow myself to be vulnerable at times like these. In crises, I was a rock. And when it was someone else's crises, I was expected to be a rock. But I didn't need cauterized emotions at this moment! I needed to *feel.*

It wasn't that I was denying or suppressing the reality. I had a vivid sense of the obvious—my mother had died, I wouldn't see her on earth again, nothing I might do could bring her back. But my mind refused to let the facts slip into my heart. Until it did, I knew my grief would be incomplete.

That's why I struggled with guilt. I loved Mom and had dreaded the day when I'd learn she was no longer with us. I woke up the next morning preoccupied with my strange lack of pain.

My brother had taken care of the plane reservations and had been able to secure us two seats on an evening flight. That meant I had a day to fill before we headed for Pennsylvania. Since my mind was so preoccupied, I decided to avoid the office, take the day off, and run some errands for Darcy.

That left me alone with a set of haunting thoughts. *Why can't I FEEL anything? Why can't I play out my grief?* As the day wore on, guilt dug a bigger hole in my soul. I needed a diversion—some place to go where I didn't have to carry the weight of my bad news on my shoulders. That's what caused me to nose my car toward Twelfth Street and Camelback. Just a little south and a little west to my favorite oasis in this desert. That's where my friend, Mike Harris, has his antique shop.

I struck up a friendship with Mike on my first visit to his little shop in Scottsdale. It had continued through his transition from little antique shop owner to the premier authority in Phoenix. But Mike's commitment to people dwarfed his enviable expertise in American antiques. If Mike were paid for being a friend, he'd be a millionaire. Regardless of when you dropped in, regardless of how long it had been since you'd last been there, regardless of whether you ever made a purchase, Mike had time to talk. I often spent a day off or a free Saturday working the strip tank or staining something for him. His shop was my therapy. I loved the smell of old wood with a new finish, of sanding sealer and Deft, of mildew and Old English furniture polish, and the constant drone of KNIX playing the latest in Arizona country music.

But mostly I just liked talking to Mike. He was a man of many subjects, many opinions, and many words. When I stopped by that afternoon, Mike and his crew were elbow deep in stain and hip deep in rhetoric. I leaned against the buffing table, listening, laughing, talking, and teasing. Mike, his wife, his son, and his assistant were experts in the banter I craved. It had a way of dissipating frustrations.

But in the middle of one of the rare lulls in the laughter, in a quiet moment, I blurted it out.

"I've got to go back to Pennsylvania."

My straight face and set eyes must have told them something was up. They all stood silently next to their work and looked at me.

"Yeah, my mom died. My brother and I are flying out tonight."

Mike's wife, Kathy, spoke first with the sensitive words that mean so much to people who have just suffered a loss. We talked for a few minutes more— the normal discussion about when, where, and how she had died. They gave me the comfort I'd come looking for, the feeling that a roomful of friends were united in their sadness for one of their own.

I stayed only a few minutes more, realizing that as long as I was there the topic was determined. I said my goodbyes and headed out to my car.

I was already inside, keys in the ignition, engine idling, clutch in, transmission in reverse when Mike came through the gate from the work area and stood in front of my car. He stood there, hands at his side, head stooped over . . . crying. He shook from deep inside of himself as tears covered his face.

The gearshift went to neutral as my grief finally shifted to drive. I stepped out of the car and Mike came over to me. He wrapped his arms around me and cried his eyes out. This man who loved to talk never said a word. He didn't need to. Besides, a library of nouns and verbs can't express what an ocean of tears from a friend can.

"Thanks, Mike."

And with those words, I drove away.

But something was different. It started in a corner of my heart and moved its way to the center of my soul. Grief. It was finally freed up to express itself. I wasn't a mile from Mike's antique store when I pulled into a grocery store parking lot to let my tears flow. Like a boxer taking a full right cross, I felt the power of loss. Mom was gone. Gone!

Then I was flooded with thoughts of a childhood spent in the shadow of a simple but superb woman. They came fast and continuously, through the waking moments of the next few days. Grief had begun to play its vital role in the repair of a broken heart.

And it all happened because a courageous friend chose to do something that didn't come naturally to him, so that I could do something I desperately needed to do.

It takes a lot of courage to be that vulnerable. To place your emotions at the mercy of someone who needs them more than you do. Mike taught me a lesson vital to love that day. Sometimes, what we do outside our area of natural strength is the most powerful thing we could possibly do. But not only that. He also taught me that one man's vulnerability can become another man's courage.

CHAPTER SIX

Courage Chooses
Its Battles Carefully

Courage should never be divorced from reason. What some people call courage is just stupidity—even when paired with good motives or good causes.

A few days ago I read a newspaper article to our children about the senseless killing of a young man at a party. Without commentary, I relayed the facts and details.

Fine Christian. Loved religious music. Was accepted to a prestigious college. Hard worker. Didn't drink. Didn't smoke. Didn't cuss. There was no doubt that this boy would make any parent proud.

It was a Saturday night. His friends wanted to go to a party that had a $3.00 cover charge for all they could drink. All but one of his friends was below the legal drinking age. They asked this Christian young man to go with them in order to drive them home after they got "hammered." Actually, this was part of what he considered his "ministry" to his friends. They refused to give up drinking, so he would accompany them to their parties so a sober driver could take them home.

They hadn't been at the party five minutes when this young man accidentally bumped into another kid. He apologized and moved on. The kid he bumped into was drunk. He was also armed and dangerous. He went out to his car, got a .22 caliber rifle and came in after him. First he held the barrel to the head of one of his friends. But when he moved it away he turned it on the Christian and put a bullet in his young chest. He died within minutes.

This young man showed great valor in several ways. He tried to disarm the drunk, he leaped away from the crowd so that if the guy did fire, it wouldn't endanger anyone else. The major point of the article was to outline what a courageous young man he was.

After I read the story, I asked my kids what they thought of this young victim. They agreed with the article that the young man was courageous. But then we went back through the events to the point where he made a choice to accompany his friends to the party. I wondered out loud if his courageous act at the party was a result of a poor choice in the first place. Was it a valid "ministry" to accommodate the illegal drinking habit of his friends? The article provided a perfect opportunity to teach a crucial principle about courage: Courage chooses its battles carefully.

We must not confuse impatience for courage.

We must not confuse rashness for courage.

We must not confuse foolishness for courage.

We cannot separate common sense from courage. Courage is prudent. It is smart strength, reasoned resolve. Courage requires shrewd judgment and a keen sense of timing. If we want our children to become courageous, they've got to know that courage engages the spirit *and* the brain before it throws the muscles into gear.

Courage might decide that the fight isn't ours, no matter how legitimate it may appear.

Let's flip open the scriptures and slip behind the curtains of an ancient throne room to learn a lesson in choosing a battle carefully. Do you remember King Josiah? He was a breath of fresh air in a royal line of stagnant reprobates. From the time of King Solomon, Judah had fallen deeper and deeper into idolatry. Families were busy leaving legacies of regret. The poison started at the top and worked its way down. The whole nation was dying from the inside out.

Then came Josiah, a gleaming star in a dark sky, a daisy in a crevice of parched ground. He embodied God's grace and gave proof that Yahweh was a God of the second chance.

The book of 2 Chronicles picks up the drama of a youthful but courageous king who wasn't afraid to do the urgent housecleaning that the sins of the Southern Kingdom demanded.

> Josiah was eight years old when he became king, and he reigned thirty-one years in Jerusalem. And he did right in the sight of the LORD, and walked in the ways of his father David and did not turn aside to the right or to the left. For in the eighth

year of his reign while he was still a youth, he began to seek the God of his father David (2 Chronicles 34:1-3).

That's the kind of man we want our boys to grow up to be. He did right and sought the Lord. His career was one of the finest in Judah's history. Not since David himself sat on the throne had Judah enjoyed the advantage of godly leadership. Now they were basking in God's blessing.

And that's what makes the end of Josiah's life such a shame, and such a waste.

Neco was the king of Egypt. He had a bone to pick with the people of Carchemish up on the Euphrates River. Josiah felt compelled to intercept the forces of Neco.

Let's give Josiah the benefit of the doubt. I'm sure he meant well. But he picked a fight that wasn't his, even after God tried to make it clear that it wasn't his.

But Neco sent messengers to him, saying, "What have we to do with each other, O King of Judah? I am not coming against you today but against the house with which I am at war, and God has ordered me to hurry. Stop for your own sake from interfering with God who is with me, that He may not destroy you."

However, Josiah would not turn away from him, but disguised himself in order to make war with him; nor did he listen to the words of Neco from the mouth of God, but came to make war on the plain of Megiddo.

And the archers shot King Josiah, and the king said to his servants, "Take me away, for I am badly wounded" (2 Chronicles 35:21-23).

Josiah was a good man. He was a godly man. But he ended his brilliant career with a foolish choice that cost him his life. He stepped over the line that separates courage from vanity.

Courageous parents must not only build courage into their children, but also help them know when it's time to exercise it. It's not wise to run the first one hundred yards of a marathon in 9.2 seconds. There's still over twenty-six miles left. Courage learns how to steward its strength. Home-grown heroes must learn how to choose their battles carefully. Let's look at a few rules of thumb that help make the process of choosing more prudent.

1. Help them know their position, and play it well.

Effective people have learned to recognize and employ their gifts and skills. Once they have defined these, they work as much as possible within that area of strength. In most cases, we want to help our kids match their strengths to the battles they choose to fight.

Suppose there was a moral dilemma at school that outraged your children. And suppose they chose to join a scream-fest between the principal and a handful of concerned students. And suppose, as a result of their verbal battle, they ended up expelled from school.

Now, we all agree that there are some issues worth taking an unpopular stand. But what if your child's greatest strength is in putting thoughts down on paper? Maybe more mileage for the cause could be gained by speaking out in the editorial section of the school newspaper (or your community's newspaper). It takes courage to do either one.

Wedding our children's courage with their natural strengths might get better results. They need to let God make the choice as to whether they need to be a martyr for the cause.

2. Help them think strategically.

We can't fight all battles at once. We can't even fight all of the battles. My mailbox gets crowded with requests for financial aid to help right a wrong. Maybe it's hunger, or oppression, illiteracy, waste, child abuse, or governmental problems.

There might be ten legitimate requests for money on my desk. I might desire to send all of them a check. But that might not be strategic. Wisdom dictates that I choose one or two close to my heart.

One of the wonderful things about teenagers is how idealistic they are (although at times their idealism can be a pain in the neck). It is during these years that they begin to focus on the injustices that surround them. It's also during these years that they can get frustrated by wanting to change everything they see wrong in their culture.

We can prepare them for a lifetime of combating injustices if we help them strategically choose the handful of battles that truly burn in their heart. I need to caution us all at this point that some of the inequities they might want to address are those they see in *us*. We can strengthen their courage many times over if we let them be used by God to point out areas where we've been wrong. In the process, we also strengthen their confidence in our love for them.

3. Show them how to take a stand tactfully.

Some people confuse rudeness or poor manners for courage. They think that outshouting a speaker with whom they disagree or heckling him in public demonstrates strength of conviction. More often than not, they're simply shooting the cause of Christ in the foot—and He already had enough holes put there. We don't need to add to them by portraying Christianity as a rigid and insensitive religion. It's one thing to be fools for Christ's sake; it's another thing to be an embarrassment.

When Push Comes to Shove

If there's a constant in this book, it's the reminder that kids pick up far more from our example than our lectures. The best way we can teach our children to choose their battles strategically is to practice this principle in the battles we pick with them.

Insisting on them passing the test of apostleship when they're ten years old, encouraging them to take on incredible odds at school, expecting them to argue the finer points of their beliefs every time their nonchurched teacher breathes a heretical word, or pushing them to stand up to the bully might sound like great advice . . . but it could be the very thing that dashes their confidence for a lifetime. We have to learn to select the areas on which to concentrate. We need to constantly remind ourselves that our children are trainees, not finished products. We need to let our instruction mix carefully with time.

We also need to carefully assess the battles we've chosen to pick *against* our children. While we may want to make the length of their hair or what is or isn't attached to their earlobes a major area of conflict, the real battle lines may lie elsewhere. If we choose to fight the wrong battles on the wrong battlefields, we could forfeit the opportunity to teach them the internal and eternal lessons that take care of the external looks. Teaching our kids to choose their battles carefully, therefore, starts with us setting the standard.

Something Is Better Than Nothing

There is one thing worse than failing to choose a battle carefully, however, and that is not choosing one at all. The world is too familiar with spectators who would rather turn a deaf ear to a travesty than lay their convictions on the line. We must be willing to be involved in some kind of effort that makes a positive difference to our world.

In my book *Legacy of Love* (Multnomah Press, 1989), I said it is essential that we have convictions. I defined convictions as, "What you're willing to die for." The point was that until we have something worth dying for, we don't have anything worth living for.

If we want to teach our children to choose their battles carefully, it would help if we could name for them some of the battles we think are worth laying everything on the line. Nobody died and left me in charge of your convictions. You have to make your own choices. But I'd like to suggest four convictions that courageous people have championed through the ages.

1. *The courage to fight for our faith.*

"The problem with Christians today is that nobody wants to kill them anymore."

Those are the sad but telling words of Jamie Buckingham. People willing to die for their faith are noted as much for their rarity as for the stands they take.

If the Christian movement kept in mind who was ultimately in charge, maybe we wouldn't fear the consequences of living out our convictions. History has demonstrated that when people of faith remain focused on the God of their faith, great things happen.

Micaiah found that out. Micaiah? He was a guy like you or me who had to choose whether to compromise his faith. For Micaiah, it was worth everything to resist compromise. If you'd like, read it for yourself in 1 Kings 22.

It had been three years since the last decent war, and the troops were getting restless. When troops get restless, kings get antsy. Ahab was both hosting and boasting. The notorious king of Israel wanted to settle a score and he wanted an ally for safety's sake. That's why he called King Jehoshaphat of Judah to join him for a conference.

"Isn't it true that Ramoth-gilead belongs to us, and yet we're doing nothing to seize it from the king of Aram?"

Maybe Jehoshaphat was wise to Ahab's ways, or maybe it was that God's Spirit burned in his heart. Whichever, he promised his support—provided Ahab got a favorable nod from Above. This request proved no problem to Ahab. He simply asked his spineless puppet prophets. In chorus, they wholeheartedly advised Ahab and Jehoshaphat to link arms and armies for battle, "For the LORD will give it into the hand of the king."

But Jehoshaphat was unconvinced. "Ahab, I was wondering. Would it be possible to seek the insight of a prophet *of the LORD?*"

Stab him in the heart, why don't you? Ahab wasn't used to the sound of wisdom and divine insight, and Jehoshaphat's request caught him cold.

"Oh, there is yet another—but I hate him, because he never prophecies anything good for me."

"Nonsense, Ahab. Let's hear what he has to say."

So they sent for Micaiah. Before he was ushered in to see the king, Ahab's messenger pulled him aside and put the squeeze on him.

"Micaiah, don't you dare mess things up. The king has his heart set on this battle. He needs this victory. And he needs Jehoshaphat with him. All the king's advisors have agreed to give the go-ahead. Don't foul this up!"

Isn't it always the same?

"Don't make waves."

"Don't buck the system."

"Play along with the status quo; it makes things nicer."

The same message that hounds men and women of truth today was trying to pin a man of God into submission. But Micaiah took his cues from God. He wasn't going to allow mere men, crowned though they may be, make him cower from his convictions.

"Whatever God tells me is what I'm saying."

When called before the kings, Micaiah stood tall.

"What do you say, Micaiah—shall we fight, or

not?" Ahab spit out his words. He detested this prophetical gnat.

"Sure, Ahab, go for it. And the LORD will give it into your hand." The lines were delivered with tongue firmly in cheek—and Ahab knew it. The sarcastic inflection was all the king needed. He exploded from his throne.

"Don't try that with me, Micaiah! I want to know exactly what the LORD told you and nothing else."

Micaiah nodded and looked around the room at the "yes men" then back to Ahab.

"All right, Ahab. I saw the army of Israel, scattered on the mountain, like sheep without a shepherd. And the LORD said, 'These have no master. Tell them to go home.'"

Ahab came to a boil. "Didn't I tell you he wouldn't say anything favorable?"

That's when Micaiah explained God had sent a deceiving spirit upon the king's personal advisors. The Lord wanted Ahab dead.

A fist came out of nowhere. Zedekiah, one of the king's lackeys, buried a full-force blow into the jaw of Micaiah.

"Is that so? God's Spirit bypassed me to speak through you?"

Micaiah spit blood from his mouth and faced his attacker. "You'll see. And you'll run on that day, but you will not escape."

Ahab was furious. He threw Micaiah in prison with orders to feed him only enough to keep him alive. He would be executed after the king's safe arrival from the battlefield.

But the biblical record tells another story.

Now a certain man drew his bow at random
and struck the king of Israel in a joint of

the armor. So he said to the driver of his chariot, "Turn around, and take me out of the fight; for I am severely wounded" (1 Kings 22:34).

A divinely guided arrow struck its mark in his heart.

I slip through the pages of history and hear the faint voices of conviction taking their stand, stating their case. And like Micaiah, I realize how desperately we need courage to stand for truth regardless of the consequences. Ours is a world run by half-truths, innuendo, and misinformation. The proud, brave, and few are tempted to succumb to the pressure.

The list of compromises scroll off the screen:
Don't let your family hold you back.
If it makes you feel good, it can't be wrong.
Charge it!
Don't be afraid to go with your urges.
This hood ornament defines your level of success.

We feel it in the board room and the bedroom, from foes and friends. It takes courage to run our lives by convictions, to endure the backlash, to endure the humiliation of standing as a lone voice. But like Micaiah, we can be confident that truth, regardless of how painful it might be, is *still truth.*

Our children choose well when they exercise courage on the battlefield of faith. And we make that choice easier for them when they have seen us consistently choosing wisely on that same battlefield all of their lives.

2. *We need courage to fight for our freedom.*

Statistics show that most people today don't believe the price of protecting freedom is worth the expense. If that form of cowardice continues to grow among the rank and file, it is only a matter of time before our freedom will be irretrievably lost.

We need to groom children who realize that freedom is priceless and that without a willingness to get involved to protect it, it will decline. Our children will know this battle is well-chosen when they see us making efforts to rectify social wrongs and helping to insure the freedom that allows us to make the effort. It's difficult to make a contribution to the cause of freedom without being highly inconvenienced, without laying something on the line. Politics, school councils, relief organizations, and social watchdog services enable us to roll up our sleeves and do something. We need to be honest enough to admit that if we are aren't willing to put our convictions on the line, there will be no line to put them on. The worst thing we can do to freedom is assume it.

3. We need courage to fight for our friends.

Jesus said it. "Greater love has no man than this, that a man lay down his life for his friend" (John 15:13).

It's scary to put your heart in a position where it could be broken. That's why it takes so much courage to be a friend. Like everything else that matters in life, friends are high-ticket items. We need to show our children that friends are worth fighting for.

I was in one of my reflective moods, quietly inspecting the changes taking place in my life. There were wrinkles in the corner of my eyes, gray hair around my temples, and my morning jog was taking consistently longer to finish. The problem was also the answer. I had just turned forty.

Darcy and I were on one of our dates, sitting in the corner of the restaurant waiting for our food. I took out my pen and started to mark lines on a paper napkin. Before I was done I had made an acceptable likeness of . . . a casket.

I slid it across the table.

Darcy peeked at it, then rolled her eyes. She knew I hadn't been taking this milestone in my life as well as I should. But this time she had read my thinking wrong.

"How many people does it take to carry one of these?"

She looked at me with whimsical eyes that said, *What is he up to now?*, but she gave the right answer. "Six."

"Darcy, if I died tomorrow, who would you call to carry my casket?" I had plenty of friends who I believed would be willing to help with this task, assuming there was nothing more pressing in their appointment book. But I didn't want those type of people carrying me to my grave. I wanted people who would drop whatever they were doing in order to drop me. Our conversation reminded me I had some work to do in the area of committed friends.

I realize this could sound morbid, but I decided I needed to start grooming my pallbearers. Certainly not because I planned on needing them any time soon. But they represent the people who have been with you through the best and the worst of times. It was obvious to me that if I wanted to have rich friendships I would have to be a loyal friend myself.

The problem is that our hurried and complicated lives make grooming our mentors difficult. But friends are essential, and we teach our children well by demonstrating how valuable they are. Friendships may bring untold hassles and inconveniences. Our children need to see us courageously enduring the costs that being a friend requires. When they see the rewards that come from consistently loving, they'll know the frustrations are worth it.

4. The Courage To Keep Your Vows

The most courageous battle we can fight for the family is the one against the forces committed to breaking it up. It would be difficult to close the chapter without mentioning the battle that rages over the sanctity and security of marriage.

Let me explain. When we get married, we're usually wrapped up in a lot of feelings—good feelings of love, commitment, understanding. We long for each other. We look forward to the sexual relationship, to setting goals as a couple, to having children, to raising those children together. There's a lot of euphoria. So far, so good.

But while we're still digging rice out of our teeth, reality pays us a visit. He may stroll up beside us along the path from the altar. Or he may simply ambush us when we're balancing the checkbook, taking grief for getting home late, listening to three children fight over two cookies, walking an infant around the family room at 3:00 A.M., or when the hand of the new secretary lingers on top of ours at the copy machine. Reality loves to let you look at your friend's nicer car, the neighbor's flatter stomach, or his wife's bigger chest. Or maybe it just wraps its fingers around your heart as you look at that sleeping partner who hasn't reached out to you in months. It has a million and one ways to strike an uneasy, unresolved chord in our heart.

From my observation, this is when a couple hits the most critical but exciting point in their relationship. It's when we come face to face with real love. Love isn't a feeling, it's not a setting, it's not some fairy tale relationship—it's a straight-from-the-gut *choice*. You only know you love when you successfully and consistently stare down the option not to.

A man comes to mind. He represents so many men I've met in my travels. At 7:00 he pecks his wife on the cheek as he exits the kitchen for the garage. She is looking her worst. She's in that thing she calls a robe, yelling at those things he calls kids. She took her make-up off the night before in order to show him why she wears it in the first place. Her hair has a bad case of "bedhead" and she's not in a great mood.

This composite husband passes a Black Velvet billboard and a co-ed jogging in place at the corner. Reflection begins. Next he breezes past a couple of pretty secretaries and gropes through the cloud of Giorgio perfume that fogs their outer office. They look even more beautiful than when he said good-bye to them the evening before. He doesn't realize, of course, that these single women only had one thing to do after they left work the day before, and that was get ready to come back today. There were no diapers, homework, piano lessons, toys to pick up, lunches to pack, football practices to watch, or midnight feedings to complete—at least not for the ones that catch his eye.

He takes his position behind his desk to ponder his predicament. Perfume wafts around the corner as he studies the picture of his wife framed on the corner of his desk. The three great kids that she bore him surround her. But his senses are working against him, and the frustrations of his busy life are weighing him down.

He looks at his wife, then sniffs the air. He looks at her again, then listens to the young voices chattering in the outer office. This time, he makes an observation, something stupid like, "Boy, she sure isn't what she was when I married her."

You want to scream in his face, "Check out the mirror, friend! Gravity located you, too."

On top of that, there is the issue of the three kids who once lived *inside* of her. Three-fourths of a year each. They've clung to her ever since. That tends to put some miles on a body.

This man is facing a test to his love. It's coming at him through the poison of comparison.

This is where real love makes up its mind.

Romantic relationships don't fare well on this test. Neither do marriages bound by goals, common interests, money, or thrilling sex. The only thing that weathers this storm is a courageous commitment to stick with the pledge we made. To look past the pressures to the promise. That's when love emerges from its cocoon and grows wings.

We want our children to grow up to be courageous adults, and we know such courage must know which battles are worth the ultimate effort. We will train them well if they see us ready to make the painful efforts to stand up for our faith, fight for freedom, develop deep friendships, and protect the sanctity of our marriage. And when they see love deepen and grow between their mom and dad, they'll know that courage is worth the risks.

The Friend Called Fear

Do not be afraid of sudden fear,
Nor of the onslaught of the wicked when it comes
(Proverbs 3:25).

I had to have been about eight years old. The exact time has been lost in the fog that hangs over the memories of youth. But the event was galvanized in my heart. At the time, my parents had five kids, and by the end of the following year they would have six. Dad installed furnaces and air conditioners full time. But the home climate needs of rural Pennsylvania didn't keep him busy enough to supply the physical needs of five growing kids. That's why he had an additional business that he operated out of our garage.

It's hard to describe, but let me give it a try. Dad manufactured metal clips of various size for use in offices or restaurants. They were from three inches to a foot long and stood on a circular metal base. If you needed a file or a menu held upright, Dad had the clip to meet your needs.

The demand for this product wasn't nearly as great as the competition. But in the late 1950s, a blue collar tradesman did what he had to do to keep his family fed.

Dad had an idea. "If we nickel-plated these clips, they'd look a lot more attractive on a table or desk." Dad knew he was priced as low as the competition, and if he was going to get more business, he'd have to "outshine" them with the esthetics of his product. The nickel-coated clips would appeal to the eye more than the steel-blue clips that he had been making.

But it would require a risk.

He'd have to gamble what little money he had in order to pay someone to do the plating for him. But Dad knew that risks were part of what turns dreams into realities. That's why he took it.

I was there the day Dad received the shipment of shiny clips from the plating company. He was right. They looked a lot better. My oldest brother, Tracy, my Dad, and the man who worked for him gathered in the back room of the shop to put a few clips together to see how they looked. The procedure was simple. A round metal base was turned upside down in a die and the clip was slipped through a hole in its center. Then you pulled a lever on the die that pressed the clip through and pinched it into place.

Dad let Tracy do the first one. He pressed it down into place. Snap. The clip snapped in two as it was pinched into the slot. Tracy tried another one. Snap. Dad tried one. Snap. Then another. Snap. Each one broke at the bend.

Anyone there would have sensed frustration building into panic. They tried to find a simple solution to the problem. They checked the die that pressed it down. Maybe they were pushing too fast or applying too much force. Every time, *snap!*

I was perched on a stool over to the side, an observer filled with anticipation and excitement. But after the first few broke, I stopped watching the process and started watching my father. Each time he heard the snap, his head dropped a little lower. Each time my brother or the assistant broke another one, Dad seemed to step further away from the work bench, as though distance could give him perspective. Finally, Dad picked up one of the shiny clips and squeezed it between his fingers. Snap. It was no use. Apparently, the plating weakened the metal just enough to cause it to give under pressure.

Dad voiced his fears out loud. What would he do now? He was counting on this idea working. He was out of resources and running out of hope.

When you're eight years old and you watch your father's dreams snap in two before your very eyes, you want to do something to make it right. My initial feeling was overwhelming pity for Dad. I knew he worked hard and I felt he deserved a break for his efforts. But the forces that deal the cards weren't cutting Dad any slack. When Dad and my brother went in the house to wash up for supper, I stayed behind in the garage, muscling the clips on the die, desperately trying to get one to work. I wanted so badly to come racing into the house with a perfect clip to make the nightmare go away. All of my attempts snapped in two.

That's when the fear set in. I was still trying when my mother called me to dinner. It was dark when I walked from the garage to the house and it perfectly matched what I was feeling. When I walked into the garage, my world was bright. Somewhere in the process, someone had shut out the lights. It was the kind of fear that strike eight-year-olds when they think the secure world they're living in is crumbling. My fear was heightened by Dad's reflective silence at dinner that night. It grew further as I saw the tears falling from my mother's eyes as she washed the supper dishes.

A sinking feeling came over me like a smoky cloud and robbed me of any ability to experience joy. And for a while, it hung over our home. Dad wasn't his hang-loose, jolly self. What were we going to do?

Times like those were made for courage.

We reach for God's gift of courage in those moments when fear squeezes us in its iron grip. We all experience moments when our chrome-plated dreams snap in two. The dreams that surround our relationships in marriage, our goals, our aspirations, our endeavors can be dashed. And when that fear sets in, we find out what we know about courage.

I learned about courage as I saw my parents regroup and restrategize their future. It didn't take long before Dad was making the most of his setback. The bounce was back in his step and the determination was back in his eyes. His courage helped dry up the tears in my mother's eyes.

Shortly after this incident our family relocated in another state. If I knew all of the facts, I have a feeling that the failed experiment had no effect on my parent's decision to relocate. It doesn't really matter. Because the fear that I felt as an eight-year-old was laid to rest by parents who understood how to leverage fear to their benefit.

Fear is the primary enemy that challenges our emotional stability. Most often, it's the fear of loss. We're afraid of losing the moment, so we forfeit the priority; we're afraid of losing the opportunity, so we forfeit the responsibility; we're afraid of losing the recognition, so we forfeit the humility. Fear never lies far below the surface of our emotions.

Our children watch from the wings, they study us as we improvise our way through the daily challenges. They hear our advice and our lectures, but what impacts them greatest are our responses to whatever scares the joy out of us. As our understudies, they must some day take center stage and play their own part. I wonder what they will have learned from us?

The Funny Thing about Fear

We fear what we don't understand. And that's why most people fear *fear*. They don't understand how it works, why it is, and what it can do for us. In this chapter, I want to help us see that fear plays a vital role in courageous hearts. Even though fear is the arch-enemy of courage, it can also be its greatest ally.

Strange, when you reflect upon it, that something so bizarre can be so basic. But such is the nature of fear.

All people fear. If we didn't, we would die. Certain things must be feared. They can kill us. We normally call this "healthy fear."

I lived my teenage years on a peninsula south of Annapolis, Maryland. When the tides were unusually high, I could hear the waves of the Chesapeake Bay breaking against the beach as I lay in bed at night. I loved the bay. Catching rock fish, or blue crabs, or digging for clams in the shallow surf. It was everything an adventurous kid could want. But I also feared the bay. Not naturally. My fear had to be instilled in me by my father. He insisted that we check the weather before we went out in our boats. If small craft warnings were up, we weren't allowed out of our cove. Dad also loved the bay, but he knew what it was capable of doing. That's why he taught us to embrace a certain type of fear that could save our lives.

But what about the plain old run-of-the-mill fear that confronts us each day? The kind we feel when we answer the phone and the caller introduces himself as Sergeant So-and-So down at the local precinct, or when the whispers make their rounds back to you and you suddenly find that the past you left at the foot of the cross is now on public display in your women's Bible study. That kind of fear crawls up our back and down our throat. We never know when it is going to lunge at us from the shadows. The difference between the courageous and the not-so-courageous is how they handle this inevitable conflict. Is it a roadblock or a detour, a consideration or the last word?

That's the choice people in London had to make during the late 1930s and early 1940s. . . .

Who Goes There—Friend or Foe?

Picture British families huddled in the catacombs of London's underground, listening to a crackling Philco sitting on the concrete ledge. Its arched mahogany case shows the wear and tear of war. But perched on its podium it stands as a symbol against the German air force.

Hitler's bombers rained their terror from Whitehall to the most remote back street of London. After months of retreating to the bowels of the city, the spirit of this great people was starting to wither. Death tolls and property losses were having their intended effect. If Hitler could crush England's resolve, he could crush England.

But his bombs could not touch the invisible radio waves that sputtered to life down below. Huddled around the radios, hundreds of Brits held their breath to hear each word. The BBC was getting through where the Luftwaffe could not. The Voice of England pierced the static and pricked British hearts. Churchill's oaken voice, weary but unbending, reminded his countrymen that they could defeat the enemy without if they refused to surrender to the enemy within.

> We shall not flag or fail. We shall go on to the end. We shall fight in France, we shall fight on the seas and oceans, we shall fight with growing confidence and growing strength in the air, we shall defend our island, whatever the cost may be, we shall fight on the beaches, we shall fight in the fields and in the streets, we shall fight in the hills; we shall never surrender. . . .[1]

Churchill knew that England's greatest enemy was fear.

Victory at all costs, victory in spite of all terror, victory however long and hard the road may be; for without victory there is no survival. . . .[2]

Let us . . . brace ourselves to our duties, and so bear ourselves that if the British Empire and its Commonwealth last for a thousand years, men will still say: "This was their finest hour."[3]

Those living in the London underground had to decide. Would their fear do what Nazi bombers could not? Or would that very fear stir the will to endure? The destruction of the Third Reich illustrates their decision.

When we consider the obstacles that want to make cowards out of our children, we realize how urgently we need to impress upon them: "Victory at all costs, victory in spite of all terror, victory however long and hard the road may be; for without victory there is no survival."

Embedded in the heart of the truly courageous is the understanding that fear is vital to victory. Those who understand this make fear their partner in life. This breaks down into two fundamental principles. Courageous people consistently practice them both. Let's take them one at a time and see how they work.

Principle Number One: It takes a greater fear to cast out a lesser fear.

Courageous people move through life making use of fear in such a way that it motivates them to their highest and best good. For example:

• Brave people fear squandering their energies more than they fear hard work.

• People who live below their means fear debt more than they fear not being able to keep up with the Joneses.

The issue isn't whether you will have fear, but whether you have the kind of fear that motivates you to courageously do what is right.

Too often, the thing that brings us down is not the situation or the challenge, but rather the lack of reasonable fear for the higher values of life. *We fear the wrong things.* We fear hassles or emotional pain or embarrassment or humiliation or someone finding out that we have feet of clay.

We accommodate our lesser fears because they make us feel more immediately comfortable.

When we do this we shift fear from ally to enemy. We don't let it work for us, but against us. What a shame. The very thing that could help us stand pulls the rug out from underneath us. How much better to let fear work *for* us. For example:

It's the fear of the consequences of sin in a friend's life that enables me to overcome the fear of confronting him or being rejected by him.

It's the fear of disqualification that helps me turn my back on the lesser fear of denying myself when facing a temptation.

It's fear of short-changing my family that overcomes my fear of having to give up selfish distractions.

It's fear of standing before God and having no excuse for squandering my gifts that triumph over my fear of the sweat and the hard work required to develop them.

As you read through that list, did the same thing dawn on you that dawned on me as I wrote them? I was soundly hit by the reality that making the kind of decisions that those scenarios suggested is a lot easier if it's the way you've been taught from the beginning.

Home-grown heroes learn the incredible power wrapped up in healthy fear. They understand this kind of fear is merely a noble expectation in disguise. That's why the apostle Paul said, "God has not given us a spirit of timidity [fear], but of power and love and discipline" (2 Timothy 1:7).

A Fear That Saved

Certain news events are impossible to forget. The images they conjure up make them as recent as yesterday's *Nightline*. Do you remember when the Air Florida jet crashed into the Potomac River? Who could forget? The stories of both the courageous and cowardly that came out of that disaster made us shiver.

Most people concentrate on the individuals who are center stage in such tragedies. We fail to realize that many courageous people work behind the scenes. Their actions are never applauded. For some, they aren't even noticed.

If you recall, on that day, the East Coast was enduring one of the worst winter storms of the year. Blizzard conditions were accompanied by sub-zero temperatures. Jets crowded the tarmac and runways, waiting for a window of opportunity to take off. But those windows were few, and so narrow that only a couple of jets could get through at a time. I've been in airplanes in those kinds of situations, and I spend the bulk of my time praying for the pilot.

One pilot that day took a severe thrashing from his passengers. These men and women were beyond restless and the flight attendants were running out of ideas. They had fed them everything on board and given them all they wanted to drink. Not only were many of the travelers drunk, but they were mad drunk. They either wanted to be "up" or "out," but they could not tolerate another minute of "stuck."

A window of opportunity opened. The tower gave the nod. The co-pilot started to breathe easier. But the pilot kept studying the buildup of ice on the wings. He had been de-iced twice. He thought out loud. "Those wings don't look good." He could feel the navigator tensing up, he caught a side glance of anger from the co-pilot. He studied the wings one more time, then made his decision.

To his co-pilot: "Inform the tower that we're going back to de-ice."

"It could be another forty-five minutes!"

"Yeah, I know."

When he informed the passengers over the P.A., he could hear the profanities hurled toward the cockpit. But they de-iced, taking about twenty minutes, then took off ten minutes later.

According to company policy, when they landed safely at their destination the pilot took his position outside the door to the cockpit to greet his passengers as they de-planed. Most wouldn't even acknowledge his presence. Some groaned disgust as they slipped by. A handful went out of their way to hurl insults.

He took them without reacting. He knew what they didn't know and wouldn't know until they got near a newspaper or broadcast. In a cockpit several planes back in line, a pilot succumbed to the fear of waiting. He chose to submit to time pressures without considering the implications of his choice. A few seconds after his plane lifted off of the runway at Washington National Airport, some of his passengers were on their way to eternity.

Two pilots, two choices, two consequences. One let a greater fear cast out a lesser fear and lived to tell about it. We need to allow greater and nobler fears to overwhelm the lesser and destructive. And when our children happen to be looking over our shoulder, the results can pay off for a lifetime.

The Second Half of the Equation

Letting a greater fear cast out a lesser fear is but half of the equation. The second is like unto it:

Principle Number Two: Make fear your friend or it will become your enemy.

It may sound crazy, but we should welcome fear. I don't mean we should go looking for nightmares just so we can experience fear, but we should see fear for what it is. Fear tips us off that there is a problem and it reminds us that we're going to face choices. When we discipline ourselves to view the situation from the proper perspective, we can actually make fear our friend. In fact, *those who are willing to risk fearing are those least likely to fear risking.*

They are also the individuals most likely to pass on a courageous heritage. Home-grown heroes need to watch fear being mastered.

Leveraging Fear

It was Canada. It was cold. I had just left a session where I had been a guest speaker. I was outside but racing across the campus to get to the warmth of my room. I wasn't looking for distractions and I wasn't in the mood to learn new truth in the cold. But God has his ways.

A grove of trees stood to my right about fifty yards away. I happened to see a man hunched down at the base of a tree, hiding. I looked beyond him and saw another.

Then I saw the co-ed. She was clipping through the trees in a mild jog and she was going to pass by the tree hiding the first guy.

It all happened so fast. Within seconds it was all over. Before I knew enough even to yell, the man behind the tree jumped her. She was about 110 pounds, he was more like 200. He went straight for her throat. She flipped him over her shoulder, onto his back, and had her knee on his Adam's apple before he knew what hit him. The next guy came running. Airborne. She took the full thrust of his weight, rolled backward on the ground while using her feet to push his legs up over the top. He landed on his back and her momentum left her straddling his chest with her gloved hands hovering about six inches from his face, Ninja-style.

I was no longer freezing on the outside. I was frozen on the inside. *What was that? What just happened?* My head was running while my feet stood paralyzed. I couldn't believe what I had just seen.

And then, as casually as you would get up after a great dinner, the girl got to her feet and started brushing the grass and leaves off her sweater. So did the guys, although much more slowly. Then they started chatting with each other and walking toward me. I had to find out more. Naturally I stopped them to inquire.

What I had witnessed was a judo expert practicing with her friends. They had an agreement to attack her once a week. She never knew where or when. But they faithfully came after her. According to their testimony, they usually took the kind of beating I had just witnessed.

Naturally, I wanted to know how a girl could consistently overpower two men twice her size. That's when I learned a lesson about judo and fear at the same time. She made it clear that she wasn't stronger than either one of the guys and never would be—she didn't have to be. When they attacked her, she simply added their strength to hers.

"Come again?" I wasn't seeing the big picture.

"I just use my body as a lever and use the force of their momentum against them. The faster they come, the harder they fall."

Since then I've learned a little more about judo (not enough to protect myself, but enough to see how the concept relates to courage). We need to leverage fear. Turn the very thing that wants to nail us back on itself.

Friends can help us do this. Even if it's only by checking in with us at a low point to let us know they care.

The apostle Paul knew fear. And he knew the power that could be gained through a well-timed friend. Listen to his words to the Corinthians:

> Great is my confidence in you, great is my
> boasting on your behalf; I am filled with

comfort. I am overflowing with joy in all our affliction. For even when we came into Macedonia our flesh had no rest, but we were afflicted on every side: conflicts without, fears within. But God, who comforts the depressed, comforted us by the coming of Titus (2 Corinthians 7:4-6).

A friend, a family member, a mom or dad can be the catalyst needed to bring courage out of a person. We need to be the kind of leaders in our children's lives that factor in their needs and help them courageously face their fears.

There's a doctor in Fort Worth who understands how to leverage fear in a positive way. He not only works in emergency rooms, but owns several in the greater Fort Worth area. He's a superb doctor but an even greater father—great enough to be willing to take a difficult and unpopular position with his daughter.

She turned sixteen, one of the milestones in a girl's life. Among the new privileges she inherited with her birthday was the option to have a driver's license. Like her peers, she looked forward to the new freedoms her license would bring on Friday and Saturday nights.

"Dad, can I use the car Friday night?"

"Sure, hon. Just make sure that it's back in the garage by 11:00 P.M."

She thought she misunderstood him. She hadn't. Eleven o'clock was correct. But that's when most teenager's evenings are just beginning! She resisted. He stood firm.

He didn't want to break her heart or be impossible. He was merely making a decision based on his personal knowledge of what happens after eleven on Fridays and Saturday nights in his town. The statistics showed it was during those two time periods that the bulk of the accidents involving teenagers took place.

She didn't care. "I'm willing to take my chances."

"Well, I'm not." She was becoming obstinate. He was becoming desperate. That's when he decided to employ her for the next two months at one of his emergency rooms. Her hours were from 11:00 P.M. to 2:00 A.M., Friday and Saturday night. She worked side by side with him and saw firsthand why he was so rigid about the curfew. It didn't take much to convince her. When teenager after teenager came in with injury after injury, she got the point. It was chilling, a bracing slap in the face that developed a healthy fear that made her want to avoid driving the streets late on Friday and Saturday night.

You might think he was cruel. I think he was courageous. He knew that extreme measures are the only way to avoid extreme pain. Who knows, he just might have saved himself having to treat her as a patient.

Fear and courage are inseparable. One can enhance the other. Proper fears eat improper fears for lunch. If we want courageous kids, they need to see us adopt a perspective that sees past the moment, the discomfort, the rejection, and the loneliness, and past our fears to the bigger, more timeless and eternal issues. When they see us using our fears wisely, our fears can do something that we seldom imagine.

They can give them courageous confidence.

Notes

1. Winston Churchill, Speech in the House of Commons, 4 June 1940.

2. Winston Churchill, Speech, 13 May 1940.

3. Winston Churchill, Speech in the House of Commons, June 1940.

The Cost of Cowardice

"May I slip out the back?"

It was a parenthesis in my morning. I was just another busy guy, trying to squeeze some personal time into my work schedule and feeling guilty for the attempt. The day had been set aside for others—others with shoulders that shrugged, eyes that misted over easily, and hearts strained by the extra pounds of life's cares. But between appointments where people would sit in the safety of my office and pour out their hurts, I decided to run over to a frame shop nearby to pick up a print that had been matted and framed for me. I left a downpour of tears to face a downpour of rain.

The God who causes his rain to fall on the upright and the uptight without showing favoritism was over-doing it for my tastes. Wisdom dictated staying put and picking up the picture some other time. But I didn't want to wait.

That's how I found myself navigating a shopping center parking lot that looked more like a yacht club. I braked my Taurus to let a woman pass in front of me. I pictured the cornish hens in her shopping cart doing the back stroke.

It seemed that everybody wanted to park in front of the frame shop, so I circled it a few times to see if I might seize an opening. No luck.

That's how my car ended up behind the shop. I ran a lap around the building and ended up standing in spongy Weegins with a take-a-number slip running its ink over my wet fingers. Meanwhile my mind-of-its-own head of hair dripped a gallon and a half of precip down my back.

"Mr. Kimmel, your print isn't ready."

"But—it says on my work order that you'd have it done yesterday."

"It also says here, 'Because some supplies require special ordering, completion date is not guaranteed.' " She sneered the "special ordering." "Notice our phone number right after this statement." She punched out the words *phone number.* "Most people call. You should have called, especially with this weather."

From soaked to sermon. If I wasn't getting nailed by Mother Nature I was getting drilled by Mother Superior. The thought crossed my mind, *Did she go to school to learn how to frustrate people, or is it second nature to her? I pity her casual acquaintances.*

"Well, I was just anxious to see how the picture turned out."

"We would have discouraged you from carrying your picture out in this weather anyway. Moisture between the glass, it'll ruin them, you know. And we aren't responsible if you—"

"May I use your back door?"

"Excuse me?"

"My car is behind your building. May I slip out the back?"

"Oh. Because of the rain? Of course. But don't touch anything in the work room. You could get hurt and we're not responsible—"

"Right." *I pity her pets.*

While I was leaning with my back against the door, ready to throw it open and make a run for it, I saw a motto, perfectly framed, hanging on the wall over the main work table.

> *You may not have time to do it right,*
> *but you'll have to take time to do it over.*

"Be careful not to bang the door into a car that might be parked too close—and try not to let the rain in."

"Right." *I pity the air she breathes.*

From stifled to sticky, I hopped my way around the deep puddles to my car and jumped inside to its humidity. I retrieved a bank deposit receipt from under the front seat and wrote down the motto before it blurred in my memory: "You may not have time to do it right, but you'll have to take time to do it over." There was something timely about those words. As I made my way back to the office leaving a wake behind, I thought of how well they fit the people on my schedule that morning.

One couple had failed to set and maintain

boundaries for their son while he was little. Neither were good at confrontation. Now their son was big and unbridled—and holding his parents as emotional hostages. They wanted wisdom on how to instill restraints and discipline. Unfortunately, I didn't have a magic wand.

A husband with unchecked rage was trying to find out how to win back the wife he had beaten. After half a dozen poundings her body and her spirit had had enough. In the process of telling me his dilemma he played the game of self-denial that put him in this nightmare in the first place. This yuppie husband with the corporate world by the throat didn't have the courage to be honest with himself. He took the coward's way around the rage in his heart, and when it seized his soul he exploded—lashing out at those he loved. He thrashed a woman half his size because of a cowardly streak twice his size.

Waiting for me at the office was a young man who had indulged his libido ever since puberty. A string of broken-hearted girls and years of regrets were finally catching up with him. He wanted help in healing the hurts that he had given as well as received. He had scorned the rebukes of the youth pastor about his promiscuity, he had laughed at the naive fathers who actually trusted him with their daughters, and he had kept the notches on his dashboard gleaming with Armor-All. Behind the chiseled jaw and the Chippendale physique, however, was a little man with the willpower of a wimp. He was nursing a heart full of regrets. The biggest one was a baby who ended up in a dumpster at the abortion clinic.

"You may not have time to do it right, but you'll

have to take the time to do it over."

People who I cared for were finding out the cost of cowardice. They were having to take the time to do over what they were supposed to do right the first time. For some, the damage was beyond simple repair. Parking my car and running for my office, I thought of how expensive it is to be a coward. I was learning firsthand from people, well-meaning people, who couldn't face their fears in one or two areas of life.

It takes a lot of courage to apply regular direction, boundaries, and discipline to a child. It takes a lot of courage to get help curbing the rage within you that would cause you to pummel the innocent and unprotected. It takes a lot of courage to admit you're a taker rather than a giver—that you want love without having to assume any responsibility for it.

That's why we need to transfer this truth about courage into the depths of our children's heart:

It costs more to be a coward
than to be courageous.

Cowardice Is No Bargain

People embrace two false assumptions when considering cowardice and courage. The first is this: *cowardice looks like a bargain.*

It isn't.

When you factor in the downside of running from our responsibilities, the price of negligence is astronomical. If we want home-grown heroes, our children desperately need to understand this.

A coward doesn't want to face the cost of applying his mind and skills to his academics. It looks cheaper to coast through school, doing the minimum of work required. But consequences will hand you a bill for laziness. The cost in dollars for those who thought they could get by with minimum effort adds up fast. How much does laziness in school cost you? Well . . . it could add up to hundreds of thousands of dollars. That's how much you could forfeit by not working your brain up to its earning potential.

A coward doesn't like to curb his passions. But the broken hearts and broken homes left behind testify to the high cost of irresponsibility. How much does infidelity cost? Ask Magic Johnson.

A coward doesn't like to bridle his anger. The scorched earth that surrounds those who refuse to exercise restraint testifies loudly to the cost of cowardice. Sometimes their cowardly nature ends up venting its rage for years—behind bars.

The Bible tells the stories of both cowards and the courageous. The high cost of cowardice leaps from its pages. The Wilderness Group thought slavery back in Egypt was easier than the price faith demanded. They paid heavily for their cowardice. David paid dearly for wanting to take the easy way out of his sin. Because of his cowardice, God said, "The sword will never leave your house" (i.e., "There will always be hostility and pain among your family").

History is largely a study of the legacy of cowards. The rare and truly courageous people grip our imaginations because they stand against the flow of events. We are impressed with the Joan of Arcs, the Isaac Newtons, the Lincolns, Edisons, and Mother Theresas. They are lilies in historical septic tanks because they were willing to take the lonely position that courage demanded. They were willing to be culture's conscience and progress' dreamers. Contrast them with some of the disasters of history, and you can see how quickly cowardice runs up a hefty tab.

My imagination grabs me sometimes. I read about past events and begin to wonder what might have happened if a significant person in the historical record had taken a different direction. I think how different the world would be, for instance, if a particular monarch would have shown some grit.

I wonder what might have happened if Queen Isabella had displayed her anger against Christopher Columbus instead of biting her lip and giving him a hero's welcome. Perhaps we wouldn't have suffered the scourge of slavery that so blighted the discovery and establishment of the New World.

King Ferdinand sent Columbus off to find gold. Columbus failed to reach the land (Mexico) that was teeming with treasure. One of the reasons that the discoverer of the New World enslaved the Indians was so he would have something tangible and marketable to show for his efforts. Queen Isabella sent Columbus out for more spiritual reasons. She wanted him to take the gospel to those he found and establish Christianity on the shores of the New World.

The history books note how disappointed she was with Columbus's treatment of the Indians. She hated his enslavement of them. But she never confronted him. She didn't have the courage to confront. The coward's path she followed was very expensive for thousands of innocent and defenseless people.

Interesting, isn't it? We think cowardice is cheaper even though repeatedly the facts show it isn't. It doesn't stop the average person from continuing to take shortcuts and half measures. It's part of our ATM/drive-thru mentality. We assume that quicker is better, time is money, easier is efficient. We don't think we have the time to do it any other way, so we leave to the next generation the responsibility of doing over what we should have done right the first time.

- The small lie looks like a cheap way out of a mistake. There's a new problem, though. Now we have to catalog that lie and file it for future reference so we can keep our deception straight.

- We keep crunching the numbers in our datebooks to make room for clutter in our schedule. If something has to go, it's our morning jog, our quiet time with God, our realistic bedtime, a decent eating schedule. When we're lying in the ICU wing of the hospital, the words coming from the blurred face of the doctor hovering over us sink in to our consciousness: "If you want to live, you are going to have to completely reformat your crazy schedule. This thing you had this morning was a warning shot. The next one's going to blow your aorta off of the top of your heart."

- The pressures of life are starting to suffocate you. What you need is a network of supportive friends to help you through your tough times. But that takes a lot of effort. Friendship is give and take—it demands large quantities of vulnerability. Why do all that work when a couple of cocktails can do the trick? So you hang out with Jim Beam, Old Grandad, and a Russian named Smirnov. It doesn't take a genius to total up the price tag on that coward's way out.

- You find birth control pills in the top drawer of your fourteen-year-old's dresser. You know she has been hostile and defiant. But you act like you didn't see anything and hope that nothing happens.

- Your five-year-old throws an embarrassing tantrum in the checkout line. You know you should deal specifically and appropriately with the real issue, but you're too embarrassed. So you surrender to his wants and buy your way out of the uncomfortable situation.

You may not have time to do it right, but you'll have to take time to do it over.

Cowardice consistently costs more than courage Which is why we should avoid it at all cost. It takes without giving until it's squandered all our emotional reserves.

I mentioned some examples from the Bible and the history books. How about yesterday's newspaper? If courage could have wedged its way into certain events, I have a feeling that today wouldn't be as painful, and tomorrow would be a lot more secure.

Let's go back again. But instead of centuries, let's subtract only a few years. I wonder about the outcome if a particular woman had taken a different stand. The following scenario NEVER HAPPENED, but in my heart of hearts, I wish it had.

"Norma, you can't do this to us."

Norma stared at the team of lawyers for a long time before she spoke. When she did open her mouth, the words came only with a struggle.

"When we began this case, it was one woman wanting to rid her life of an overwhelming responsibility. I was single, pregnant, and at a dead-end. You people surrounded me and fought for my right to decide whether to have a baby. When the Texas courts upheld the state's anti-abortion law, you pushed for the series of appeals that got us to this point. But somewhere, early in this whole conflict, it slipped from a case about me, to a case for all women. You've made me a symbol. But I'm not the same. And I don't feel the same way I did when this all began."

"Listen, Norma, we understand that you've been under a lot of stress. It makes sense that this could all be overwhelming. Maybe you just need some time to rest. We promise you that as soon as this is over, you can disappear. No more pressure, no more hounding."

"I'm obviously not making myself clear," Norma responded. "Let me try again. You see, I felt that baby kick me. I heard her cry when she came from my womb. I felt the detachment when I signed the papers that gave her to the adoption agency. I longed to hold her, to smell her baby skin, to look deep into her innocent eyes. This case is not good."

"Nonsense, Norma! Now listen, we are proceeding as planned. The Supreme Court is going to hear our case in a few minutes and this will all be history in a few days."

"Well, you're doing it without me."

"Norma, don't be ridiculous."

"You call it ridiculous—but I feel there is a fundamental question we have refused to ask."

"And what is that?"

"You really want to know? Alright. Here it is. The question is, can we absolutely, positively, and scientifically prove, beyond a shadow of doubt, that the fertilized egg in a woman's uterus is *not* a human life?"

"Norma, we've been through this a million times. How can you define life? What's human?

When does it all begin? Nobody can absolutely, positively prove that fetal tissue is or it isn't human. So what's the big problem?"

"Here's the problem. Let's put it this way. Suppose you were deer hunting. You see a large bush about fifty yards away. Its limbs are thrashing and shaking and dust is flying from the base. Something *big* is in there. Do you fire your rifle into that bush and kill what's there?"

"Well . . . no. You can't shoot until you're certain it's a deer."

"Why?"

"Well, because. It . . . it might be a *person* in the bush."

"Right!"

The tap of the court attendant on the door of their private counsel room told them their time was up. The gavel would fall any second.

"Norma, it's time."

"I know. And it's probably too late to stop what I've started. But until I can absolutely, positively be certain there is no baby in the womb, I don't want to give doctors a license to kill. Until we can prove otherwise, I believe the rights of the woman must bow to the possibility of human life in her womb. That's why I'm out of this case."

"You're a fool, Norma."

"Well, this fool is going outside and find a news crew and give them an exclusive interview on why the woman behind *Roe v. Wade* believes the Supreme Court justices are about to make a tragic mistake—for women, for children, for everyone. And after I finish it, I think I'll walk down to the Lincoln Memorial, sit on its front steps and think about a little girl who is running and playing in the back yard of her adopted home. God bless that little girl!"

This scenario only happened in my mind. Because it never happened in reality, our nation has borne the scars and responsibility for the deaths that followed the Supreme Court's decision. I am confident that if Norma had taken a stand like this, the abortion movement would have been seriously undermined regardless of *Roe v. Wade.* The coward's way out may look like a bargain, but over and over we see the net cost of convenient paths tally up higher than we could imagine.

Courage Is Not Too Expensive

We have seen that although cowardice looks like a bargain, it isn't. But another false assumption often keeps us from doing what we should: *Courage looks too expensive.*

It isn't.

Thousands of examples could prove this point, but let's look at just one. The last few pages of any of the Gospels provide the ultimate example. One drama stands out as proof that courage turns out to be the most personally profitable option people can choose. Because of the players who surround this event, it also illustrates the high cost of cowardice.

Just introducing the two players gives away the ending. Respectively, they embodied courage and cowardice, faith and fear, confidence and compromise. They were Jesus and Judas. In all of history, no single story defines courage nor demonstrates the high cost of cowardice so completely as the story of these two companions.

Let's try to admire Judas for a moment. After all,

his attraction to the Lord came from deep convictions about the plight of God's people. Sick of the oppression of Rome, Judas took up with Jesus for noble reasons. His inclusion in the twelve was not from inspiration as much as aspiration. Judas was a man driven by a deep political agenda.

But he fought a battle with his dark soul from the beginning. Behind his rhetoric was a selfish heart. A little voice whispering in his brain snared and tripped him throughout his three years with the Savior.

"What's in it for me?"

Each choice Jesus made was weighed in the balance of Judas's selfish soul. Each Messianic lesson on generosity and sacrifice fell dully on the floor of Judas's larcenous heart. Try as he might, he could not see past his own ego to Jesus' plan to redeem a fallen world. When the push of public sentiment came to the point of shoving, his spirit willingly slithered further into the black hole that had tugged at him all of his life.

Let's try to pity him for a moment. The twisted corpse hanging at the end of a rope once held the heart of a zealot. That zealot once nursed on a proud mother's breast. Judas, the betrayer, had once incarnated a father's dreams. In many ways, he was the most qualified of the twelve to be a disciple. He loved his country, he wanted freedom for his people, and he was willing to put himself in jeopardy to see those dreams come true.

I doubt that few disciples stepped up to accept Jesus' offer with the enthusiasm or the expectation of Judas. Finally, a liberator of the people! A man who would take on Rome! For Judas, Jesus personified everything he had longed for.

That's why the last chapter of his life stands as such a pitiful commentary to the wages of cowardice. Judas is proof that credentials don't determine commitment and passion alone cannot overcome pressure.

Somewhere between casting his lot with the Savior and casting it with Satan, Judas had shifted from student to scrutinizer, from disciple to deceiver, from truster to traitor.

It was the night before Passover. Hands that would be blood-stained by morning gently bathed feet that would run to make it so. Then supper time. Time to reflect, to remember the promises of God who delivered His people. All that Judas had dreamed of was reclining next to him at the supper table; but his dreams had become clouded by ultimate cowardice.

Eleven men huddled around Jesus, mentally rehearsing the events he memorialized with the familiar words of the Seder. One did not. In the flickering shadows crouched the vile spirit of darkness that had stalked Judas to this moment—waiting to pounce on the man's compromised heart. Jesus forced that heart to a vote.

"I tell you the truth, one of you is going to betray me."

Judas feigned shock and then confusion. "Who would do something like that?" He joined in the search for the traitor.

But Jesus knew. "It is the one to whom I give this piece of bread when I have dipped it in the dish."

The custom went something like this: the master of the feast would take small bites of lamb and arrange them on a piece of unleavened bread. He then would dip them in the bitter herbs and pass them to the guest. It was the custom to extend the first piece to the most honored guest. By extending this first piece to Judas, the Savior was letting him know there was still time to change his mind.

Courageous or coward? The choice was made. Barely half a day after Judas rejected Jesus' gift of escape, the cost of cowardice had been tallied up. Midday Friday, two erstwhile friends were hanging from timber. Courage hung from the cross of salvation. A coward swung from the tree of regret. In the end one drew all men to himself. The other became a byword for betrayal.

It takes a lot of courage to transfer courage to our children. If we take the coward's way out, we run up a bill we can't afford to pay.

Tallying Up the Cost

John was a budding teenager whose parents had labored to build into their son the characteristics that mark a courageous life. His childhood friends were maturing into young adulthood at the same time he was. But something was missing in them. They started taking shortcuts early in childhood. Which is why they were unable to earn a place in the concert orchestra at high school. Which is why they spent the bulk of their time watching varsity football in a clean uniform perched at the end of the bench. And which is why they consistently had to attend summer school.

John began to notice their friendship was changing, and not for the better. Once they went through puberty, the only thing his two friends had to say about girls was sexual and demeaning. Their vocabulary had taken a nose dive, too. Whenever John dared to voice his concern, he encountered a barrage of scorn and mocking. These were his friends, but it was impossible to take a neutral position when it came to the moral choices the friendship was imposing on him.

The ultimate test came one Friday night. They had driven to a remote beach to build a fire and talk. One of his friends brought a girl along. They weren't far into the evening when his friends brought the six-packs out of the trunk. The girl popped open the first can and started chugging it before the other guys had a chance to toast the evening. John declined the offer.

"Don't tell me, let me guess! The pope is declining the offer to imbibe!" They mocked their friend for his refusal to join their drinking. Their sneers informed the girl what they thought about his attitude toward alcohol. "St. John, here, has been sober since the moment the doctor slapped his sanctimonious rear end." She accentuated the mockery by pouring beer down the front of her clothing and inviting him to "reconsider." It was all the prompting his friends needed. The conversation and the evening took on a sexual focus that could only lead in directions John knew were dangerous to his soul. The only solution for him was to leave. But they were a long way from home.

He volunteered to drive if they would let him get close enough to a phone to call his parents for a lift home. One friend laughed so hard that he fell backward off the log he was sitting on. "Nothing doing. We came here to get drunk and nothing's going to stop us. Give it up, John, it's just a matter of time before you'll wake up to the reality that life isn't as black and white as you think." John's parents had taught him well that life was cluttered with ambiguities, but this scenario wasn't one of them. That's when he made the courageous decision to walk home. Going back the way they got there was the shortest, but most dangerous. Most of it was through the woods. The longest but safest way was the beach.

Their laughter faded in the distance as he headed for home. He jumped jetties and waded under piers, encountered a couple of unhappy dogs and one narrow inlet (which he swam) before he came to the part of the peninsula that led to his community. He was in bed by curfew, and deep asleep at the height of his friend's evening.

He wasn't there when his friends lost their virginity. He wasn't there when they fumbled around looking for the keys to the car in the sand. He wasn't there when they stopped in the woods so that the girl could throw up. He wasn't there when they left her propped against a stop sign near her house. He wasn't there when they drove their car into the tree at a knee in the road less than a mile from his home. And he wasn't there . . . when they died.

The article in the paper talked about the series of mistakes that culminated in the death of the two boys. It never mentioned that it could have been three young men who died. It didn't really matter. The most important thing remained true regardless.

John was alive. His two friends weren't.

Our children will face a lifetime of opportunities to take the coward's way around a dilemma. Someday, they'll be short on cash when the opportunity comes for them to take what doesn't belong to them. They will have hundreds—maybe thousands—of opportunities to build themselves up by tearing an associate down. And shunning the lusts of the flesh will take a stronger resolve than any of us parents could ever imagine as our culture becomes more X-rated.

Don't think that their faith will get them through this. Only *courageous* faith will. Don't think that their values will get them through this. Only courageously embraced values will survive. Don't think that their convictions will stand up to the test. Only convictions strengthened by down-deep-in-your-soul courage will endure. That's why Sunday school and family devotions aren't enough. Courage isn't learned in the lecture hall but in the laboratory. And each day provides the perfect backdrop for modeling and transferring courage.

Yes, courage costs. But cowardice costs more. I know of at least two tombstones that make that abundantly clear.

The Commitment
to Courage

And let us not lose heart in doing good,
for in due time we shall reap if we do not grow weary
(Galatians 6:9).

It was a rare night. The waves washed the beach in endless, haunting rhythm, lit by a three-quarter moon.

It was a rare opportunity. My schedule seldom concedes time for such things as moonlit walks along the beach at Malibu.

It was a rare conversation with a good friend. Mark, though younger, has become a great mentor to me. He has a practical brilliance that feeds my soul.

And it was a rare moment of personal honesty. When forced to ponder a point in the conversation, I realized how much we are dependent on courage to keep our vows in marriage.

We had been discussing Mark's worries about matrimony. He "thought" he was in love, and wanted to ask her The Question. But he was paralyzed by a fear that brought him up short of commitment.

We had talked around the subject for about an hour. Finally I pinned him for the truth.

"What's holding you back, Mark? If you think she's the one, and you feel the time is now, why don't you go ahead and ask her?"

Maybe it's my tendency to make things as uncomplicated as possible, but it seemed to me that all of the normal barometers a person checks before they take the plunge indicated he couldn't pick a better time to at least ASK. He was educated, gainfully employed with good financial depth (which isn't a necessity for wedlock, but certainly didn't hurt), and the girl he loved loved both him and Him. What was the problem?

"Here's what's holding me back."

I slowed my steps in order to concentrate on his words.

"I'm afraid that I'll marry her, then afterward I'll wonder if I made the right choice. By then it will be too late. I want to make absolutely sure—no doubts in my mind—that she is the one before I risk it all."

It wasn't fair to laugh at him. After all, he was sincere and genuinely wrestling with his fears. But part of me had to laugh. Not at him. At me. I remembered feeling the same concerns almost two decades earlier when I was wrestling with the same question.

As I pondered it now, I figured it was probably part of the process of proposal. The difference between me and Mark was that his uncertainty had him paralyzed and his love for this girl was being held back. So I decided on the blunt approach.

"Mark, let me relieve your worries. You need not fear if you'll regret your decision to marry after the wedding. Why fear something that is a foregone conclusion?"

"One more time, slowly."

"It's not a case of *if* you'll question it, but *when*. Mark, you will question your decision. Maybe even regret it. I did."

I explained how I had wondered, after I got married, if I was ready for the responsibility, if I was old enough, mature enough, spiritual enough. What's more, so did Darcy—not about her, but about me.

Mark was only experiencing in advance what every couple knows day by day. Love is a choice. Doubts are part of the picture. And regrets have a way of wedging their way into our moments of reflection.

Honesty forced me to confess that I had given Darcy many reasons to regret her decision to marry me. That's why I feel so loved by her. In spite of my shortcomings and flaws, she has chosen to love me.

"Mark, it takes courage to get married. And it takes a lot of courage to stay married. You don't need to worry about your doubts. You don't even need to worry about your love. All you really need is courage."

And when it comes to transferring that courage to our children, it's more a matter of "going the distance" than it is anything else. We might demonstrate occasional pockets of heroics, but for courage to move from the veneer of their personality to the core of their being, our children need to see us endure.

That requires commitment.

In this chapter I want to remind us of what we already know: *Courage requires a commitment from us as parents.* What we say will either be verified or negated by the level of commitment we demonstrate.

The chances of producing home-grown heroes diminishes proportionately with our failure to follow through on our promises. It is essential that we decide certain things at the outset. Otherwise the principles we've developed in this book will remain untried theories.

Let me mention three areas where we must make a courageous commitment. You'll notice I've mentioned them already. That's okay. Commitments in these areas are indispensable in our efforts to transfer courage to our children.

1. We need commitment to our marriages.

"I'd like to introduce you to my future ex-husband." That's just about the way it goes at the company Christmas party. We've gotten so conditioned to love NOT working out that we assume it's a foregone conclusion.

Not that anyone sets out to be divorced. But somewhere between the wedding ring and the baby's teething ring, reality muddies the sea of love that we swore we had fallen into. Gradually, we want to find out how to swim to the edge and climb out.

It takes a lot of courage to get married today. It's not just a man, woman, a plow, and a couple of acres any more. True, we gain a lot when we marry. But we also give up a lot. A lot of the good things that we gain when we get married can also complicate our commitment. Sometimes a couple doesn't have to go any further than the picture of their in-laws on the end table to know why it's so difficult to maintain their love.

The complicated relationships made at marriage altars these days tax emotions more than ever before. It isn't surprising that so many couples find coping through the frustrations of marriage too difficult. The truth is, there are enough wounds on Baby Boomer hearts to last a lifetime. If we don't do something about the fragile foundations on which our families are built, we're going to see not just one generation, but a spate of generations pay the price. The numbers don't lie. A person's chances of ending up in court jump considerably if he or she comes from a home scarred by divorce.

We need courageous partners who take on the bounced checks, receding hairline, and stretch marks with mutual resolve. Such partners not only enjoy the pure richness of love that endures the test of time, but also hand their kids the best shot at love that lasts. None of it comes easy.

2. We need commitment to sacrificial parenting.

Every parent I've ever met has been *willing* to sacrifice. It doesn't take courage to be willing to do something. It only takes courage to *carry out* the sacrifice. That's when the pressure gets the best of us. I've been there. I am there. I must choose every day whether I will stand or fall when relentless pressures pound me. Whatever pressures try to beat me down, however, they are tame next to those that buffet my wife.

Moms and dads are the true unsung heroes of the new millennium. To do their job properly, they often have to choose options that run against their internal grain.

• Will he help with homework instead of finishing a Tom Clancy novel?

• Will she cheer on a Little League game instead of hitting the mall?

• Will they wait up for their kids to get in on Saturday night instead of falling into bed?

Parenting is painful. It's rewarding, of course. But most of the payoff is so far down the road that the average parent finds it too tempting to give up.

Sacrificial parenting is a popular concept, but not a popular way of life. That's why so many people laud it but so few do it. We get sidelined somewhere in the first quarter and want to beg out of the rest of the game.

Maybe that's why I'm writing this book. It's just as much for me as it is for anyone who might read it. I have a bad habit of growing weary from well-doing. I'm like the next parent in line—if I could just go to the Hilton and sleep for a couple of months, I'd be fine. But that luxury won't be handed to me.

Just last night I wanted to get a head start on today by getting a good night's sleep. So did Darcy. I climbed into my side of the bed at 11:00 P.M. I was dreaming in five minutes. An hour later Darcy finally crawled into her side. Our nine-month-old was still crying. Not the quiet, cooing cry that often serves as a self-performed lullaby. He was testing the strength of the wall paper. Ear infections do that to babies. Darcy's presence on *her* side of the bed meant it was my turn to get out of *my* side of the bed. And I did.

Not because of some Florence Nightingale syndrome, but because there was no way I was going to be able to sleep through the baby's wails.

It was 1:15 A.M. when his breathing moved deep enough to attempt putting him back in his crib. I had put about ten miles on the rocking chair. During the hour and fifteen minutes my son fought to find a comfortable position on my chest, my mind wandered to the next day, to this moment, when I would stare at my word processor and try to give a word of encouragement to parents who want to raise courageous kids. With all the ideas swirling in my head, the one lesson that kept coming back to me is how desperately we need to have the courage to complete what we've begun.

Those Gerber babies we bring home from the hospital don't look much like the kid on the jar. They're going to give us a run for our emotional money. But of all the gifts we can give their spirits and of all the strength we can build into their lives, the best thing we can do is to not give up. Don't surrender on our teaching, our affirmation, our discipline, or our spiritual example.

3. We need commitment to carry on in hardships.

Sticking with our vows and sacrificially parenting are two ways we can teach our children courageous living. But sometimes we are called to extraordinary circumstances. Painful settings require more resolve than most people care to muster. It is in these times where we must maintain a third level of commitment.

I remember tuning in my television to news of a home-going. A single flute played a familiar tune.

No one needed to remind me of the words. They were so much a part of the melody that you couldn't hum it without thinking of their promise . . .

> I once was lost but now am found,
> Was blind but now I see.

Ryan White lay in the wooden casket, finally resting after years of struggling for understanding and compassion. He was a mother's pride, brought down by the vicious virus that causes AIDS. As the notes played, America wept for a little boy who had been punished too long.

Six years earlier, hemophilia required that Ryan receive a transfusion to thicken his blood. Unknown to anyone until it was too late, Ryan was given blood that began his march to the grave. Before that death would finally overtake him, he would have to suffer the public humiliation that accompanied a stigmatized and misunderstood disease.

Frightened people do insensitive things. Once it became public knowledge that Ryan had AIDS, he was treated as if he wore a scarlet letter. Nice people, people like you and me, found it hard to believe the doctors when they said the virus couldn't be transmitted by proximity or through the air. Ryan's classmates, the doctors assured, were in no danger.

But the emotional and social attacks continued.

Ryan came home from school to show his mother a file. Someone had scrawled the word "Fag" across the front. It was one of many cruel ways that people told a little boy he wasn't wanted. "He spit on me!" one kid falsely accused. "He took a bite out of a cookie and put it back." It was another of many hateful accusations he had to endure. Finally a vote was called and the boy was banished from school.

When a parent suffers unjustly it's tough. When a parent has to stand by helplessly and watch a child suffer, the pain is excruciating. Both Ryan and his mother were hounded by a community that didn't understand the illness. In an effort to protect themselves the townspeople spurned a family in desperate need of compassion.

What ultimately turned a nation's sentiments around was not information, or education, but the testimony of a young man who endured without retaliating and a mother who coached her son to move beyond rage. Ryan believed enough to be able to forgive, refusing to carry a weight of bitterness to his grave. In the fourth quarter of his brief life, people reconsidered. He was brave, tolerant, and wise beyond his years.

A winsome little boy faced death with a courageous heart. Hand in hand with his mother, he deflected the fears and the threats, the accusations and the ridicule. Ultimately, he won his place in a nation's heart.

In a way he was a metaphor. He illustrated the human dilemma and the divine solution. Ours is not a world that takes easily to compassion and understanding. We bite before baring our teeth. We do both before we think.

It's the same madness that causes the yuppie to roll down the window of his BMW and scream at the homeless family next to the dumpster to clear out of his neighborhood. We want to stay insulated from other people's hurts.

But every once in awhile a little voice in the

back of our spirits whispers a question that echoes in our soul . . .

What if it were you? What if that were your child?

It's not until it gets unavoidably close that we step from the protection of our comfort zones and actually do something.

I remember taking the call from my brother Todd announcing the birth of his second child, Jessica. It was a rarity, a girl in a family tree crowded with boys. I rejoiced with him and his wife, Ruthie.

I remember taking another call from him several months later. Something was wrong. No one knew the cause, or the solution, but Jessica was fighting severe seizures—a consequence of inexplicable brain damage.

It takes a lot of courage to reformat your lives. It takes a lot of courage to accept, without complaint, the responsibility of raising a child who may never be able to feed herself, comb her own hair, read a book, or walk down an aisle to a bridegroom.

In those rare, transparent moments when Todd lets his weary guard down, he tells me of his frustration at people who should know better. He tells me how difficult it is to hear the well-meaning but misguided say things like . . .

"Listen, you have to suck it up and endure. This is what God intended and you have got to accept it."

"Put her in some hospital and let them take care of her. Why hold yourself hostage?"

Words from moms who have never had to carry a child half their own weight to the bathroom, who have never had to sing lullabies to a girl who can't express her joy, who have not had to find out what it's like to go six years without a decent night's sleep. Words from fathers whose daughters run to meet them when they get home from work, who play Little League and jump rope and dream of what they'll wear for their prom. Unless some breakthrough occurs, Jessica won't know what a baseball is, or a jump rope, or a prom.

Yet Todd and Ruthie refuse to complain. Nor do they look for an easy out. That's why the lectures from comfortable friends cut so deeply. He said to me one time, "Jesus doesn't give us a cross which He won't help us carry." For my good brother and his good wife, Jessica may be an extremely heavy cross, but they see her as too much of a gift to be a burden. And when I hold that little girl close to me and rest my chin next to her soft face, I remember Jesus gathering the children around him and reminding the disciples, "Encourage little children to come unto me, and don't refuse them access, for they represent the very soul and spirit of my Kingdom."[1]

Courage cuts through rhetoric. It sees past hip braces and walkers, catheters and bedpans. It acknowledges the prejudice and fear within and the needs without.

Convenience sees a little boy dying of AIDS and permits its prejudice to turn away from him. Courage sees that same boy and enfolds him in compassionate arms.

Convenience sees a man and woman foraging through a dumpster to find enough food to feed their kids and screams at them to get lost. Courage finds a way to get them a decent meal and show them a way to a better and safer life.

Convenience sees a young mom carrying a

fifty-pound child and says, "I'm glad it's not me." Courage comes alongside and helps her carry that child through life.

For those who step over the lines of prejudice, of fear, of inconvenience, there is a personal reward:

> "Come, you who are blessed of My Father, inherit the kingdom prepared for you from the foundation of the world. For I was hungry, and you gave Me something to eat; I was thirsty, and you gave Me drink; I was a stranger, and you invited Me in; naked, and you clothed Me; I was sick, and you visited Me; I was in prison, and you came to Me."

> Then the righteous will answer Him, saying, "Lord, when did we see You hungry, and feed You, or thirsty, and give You drink? And when did we see You a stranger, and invite You in, or naked, and clothe You? And when did we see You sick, or in prison, and come to You?"

> And the King will answer and say to them, "Truly I say to you, to the extent that you did it to one of these brothers of Mine, even the least of them, you did it to Me" (Matthew: 25:34-40).

Courage is a choice, a difficult choice often wrought with pain. But it is a choice that comes with a blessing and a reward. Parents willing to make the choice to commitment not only receive the blessings and the rewards, but they pass them on as a gift to the next generation.

As I reflect on the courage it takes to keep a commitment, I always flash back to a scene from years ago.

It was in the Smoky Mountains—1968. My first year of college, my first time away from home, and my first look at the ravages known as Appalachia. I studied in a tree-covered oasis, a pocket of Southern comfort surrounded by some of the poorest counties in the country. My education would ultimately pull me off of the hill and force me to confront the needs around me.

A few weeks after I started classes, I met a senior majoring in theology. Committed to being a pastor, David wasn't waiting for graduation to get a church. He and his wife were working at a small parish in the county north of us.

Perhaps I showed too much interest or perhaps it was David's persuasive words, but before I knew it I was in his car squeezing the door handle as he negotiated the switchbacks that would eventually drop us into a remote village in Roane County, Tennessee. His new Sunday school teacher was green around the edges when we finally arrived.

David was a romantic. Which explains why what he described and what I found waiting for me were so far apart. First, he had oversold the village. There was a house, a ramp for loading cows onto a truck, and an unpainted rectangular building with a primitive steeple. As I sized up the three structures, it looked like the cattle got the best treatment. Second, he had oversold the people. I had grown up in a rural setting and thought I knew country folks. But these were extremely poor, mountain folks. It wasn't just the way they appeared on the outside. They had on their best clothes, which, for some of them, were their only clothes. Poverty had quenched the fire on the inside. These were a beaten down people.

There was one Sunday school room and the main room where we would meet for services. I was to teach in the small room. There were seven kids ranging in age from nine to seventeen. After David made his brief introduction, they were all mine. I stepped to the front and smiled at them individually. Each one stared blankly at me—except one. He looked away.

I focused on the oldest, a boy.

"Hi. What's your name?"

Nothing.

"My name is Tim."

Nothing.

I looked at the next one.

"What's your name?"

Nothing.

"Would anyone like to volunteer his name?"

Nothing. Expressionless eyes stared at me.

I tried an anecdote about growing up in a large family.

No response.

The room was thick with humidity and I was getting worried. I hoped a diversion might help.

"Listen, it's so nice out today. Why don't we take our chairs outside and sit under the tree?"

No words were spoken, but they stood up and proceeded to drag three chairs and a bench outside. One of the older kids automatically grabbed the nine-year-old's chair and carried it for him.

"This is much better. Now, who can tell me the story about the boy who fought the giant with a slingshot?"

I figured we'd start with the familiar. Few kids make it through childhood without learning of David and Goliath.

Nothing. Just stares and emotionless faces.

So it went for fifty-five minutes—the longest fifty-five minutes I could remember. A man stepped outside the church to catch a smoke before the worship service. One last try . . .

"Would anyone like to thank Jesus for our time together?"

No one wanted to. Neither did I. But I went through the motions anyway, thanking the Lord for each one of them.

"Okay, take your chairs back into the room, and I'll see you next Sunday."

I lied. I wasn't about to go through this again and I figured I'd tell Dave when he dropped me off at my dormitory. On the way back, we small-talked about the kids, their parents, and school before he pulled up in front of my dorm.

"Dave, listen. I need to tell you something—"

"You don't want to go back?" His tone was matter-of-fact, not accusative.

"It's not that, but . . . well, you're right, I don't want to go back."

"They didn't say a word to you, did they?"

"No. Not even their names—"

"They can't."

"You mean those kids can't talk?"

"They can talk alright. But not to you—not to anyone from the outside."

"I don't get it."

David went on to explain the broken spirit of these people. It was a combination of poverty, no opportunities, and little education. They were economically retarded. To complicate matters, these children were offsprings of families who had interbred for decades. Most, if not all, were mildly damaged in their ability to learn and communicate.

Then he gave me the choice that would become one of my better lessons in finishing what I started.

"Tim, it's up to you. No guilt trip, no sermon. I could use you up there. The kids need someone to be there. You give it some thought and let me know before next Saturday night."

I saw him Tuesday and agreed to give it another try. But he caught me off-guard.

"Unless you're going to commit to the whole year, it would probably be better that you don't go back. It wouldn't be fair to the kids to get them attached and then drop out."

"Attached! Are you kidding, David? It's like teaching a salad bar!"

"You're teaching children whom Jesus died for."

The rebuke was deserved and accepted without argument. Everything inside of me said no. Logic said no. My schedule said no. But ultimately I said yes.

And every Sunday for my first year of college I met David and his wife at 7:30 in front of the dorm and drove off through ground fog and purple haze to the kids. I learned their names from some of the adults who brought them and made it a point to say hello to each one by name every Sunday. I also taught them a different lesson every Sunday, spending most of my time in biblical narratives. I shared the gospel story and prayed a prayer for anyone who might want Jesus in their heart. I peeked during my prayer. Each had their head bowed, but they were all looking at me.

I taught Sunday school at that church from the second week in September 1968 to the third week of May 1969. And in that time those children said a grand total of . . .

Nothing.

They never said one word.

David was graduating and going on to seminary. I had been recruited to help a man with a little country church north of Chattanooga, a church I would end up pastoring my last two years of college. For my last Sunday, I decided to forgo the lesson and just talk about my family and life back in Annapolis, Maryland. I told them about the Chesapeake Bay, my high school, my girlfriend back home, and a little about the college I attended. The last thing I said to them was that I hoped they had a nice summer. And, of course, I got no response.

Thinking back across the decades, I often wonder what God was trying to teach me during my time with those kids. I picture myself out under that tree, acting out the David and Goliath story: swinging an imaginary sling, picking a rock from the grass and placing it between my eyes, then falling backward, imitating Goliath's famous death scene. Then lifting my head up to see seven expressionless faces staring at me. I think of the time I climbed the tree and pretended I was tiny Zacchaeus trying to get a better look at Jesus as he passed by. Seven sets of eyes stared up into the tree, indifference written all over their faces. I think of all the coats, sweaters, and shoes that David and his wife brought to the people during the winter months, and how the kids would slip them on, sit in their chairs, and stare at me as I went through the motions of teaching.

Probably what God wanted me to learn more than anything else is that you finish what you start. I know full well that had David not continually talked me into it, I never would have lasted past October. He kept reminding me that you don't base your decision to serve on the results of your service. You do it because it's what God requires.

I have to say that if it was nothing else, it was good practice for parenting. It seems I'm forever teaching the same lesson to expressionless faces:

"You forgot to brush your teeth."

"Don't hit your sister."

"Look at me when I'm talking to you."

"How do you ask for a drink of apple juice?"

And on and on. We think they're not hearing a word we say. After reminding them for the five thousandth time to flush the toilet when they're done, we simply want to give up.

David finished preaching his sermon the last Sunday I was there. The kids sat among their parents like they always sat—expressionless, emotionless. After the sermon, they went out and huddled near the cattle trough, where they huddled every Sunday after church.

We chatted with the adults and then headed to the car. I waved over toward the kids, but they weren't looking at me.

And then it happened. I had thrown my Bible in the back seat and was taking off my sports coat before I climbed in for the stuffy ride back to school. They came out of nowhere. I was chucking my coat through the back window and preparing to open the door when I felt these arms wrapping themselves around me. All but two of them were there—hanging on like they'd never let go.

I didn't know what to do, so I just stood there hugging right back. We hugged for maybe twenty-five to thirty seconds and then they stood back. I touched each one individually and tried to wish them something special.

"Hope you catch a lot of fish," to the older kid.

"Hope you get to go with your daddy to Knoxville," to the ten-year-old girl who always sucked her thumb. On down the line until I had touched the last one.

I got into the car and watched them as we drove off. They never waved, or smiled, or showed any expression. They didn't have to. Without saying anything, they had said everything.

I don't know. Maybe the real lessons in life aren't the spoken ones after all. Maybe our words are merely a sideshow to our life and only take on meaning after we've gone the distance.

Note

1. Matthew 19:14, author's paraphrase.

CHAPTER TEN

Courage Remembers Who's Ultimately in Charge

*Now to Him who is able to keep you from stumbling,
and to make you stand in the presence of His glory
blameless with great joy, to the only God our Savior,
through Jesus Christ our Lord, be glory, majesty,
dominion and authority,
before all time and now and forever.*
Amen
(Jude 24-25).

I've observed thousands of teenagers from
every kind of home take on the best and worst that
life can dish out. Those who maintain their convictions and willingly resist the pressure of the world to

compromise can be cataloged under one heading: Security.

IQ doesn't cut it.

Success-grooming makes no difference.

They can have shelves crowded with trophies and heads cluttered with ideals. But unless a deep sense of security pervades their lives, they can't handle the pressures that inevitably come.

If our children are to become courageous, they need to have confidence in Someone greater than the challenges they will face.

Our kids need to know that God is, that He has spoken, and that He has the power to enable them to face their fears. God is to be the foundation of their confidence and it is on this foundation that we must seek to build their lives.

Young people need a relationship with God that isn't weighted down by worn-out liturgies or pop sermons that offer hope without truth. Our kids don't attach to beliefs that are all dessert, and no vegetables. What they need is to be introduced to a faithful God.

Faithful. It's one of the all-time best words in the dictionary. It shouts, "You can count on me!" And that is exactly the kind of God you find in the Bible.

Ultimate Security

As parents, we cannot control all of the circumstances in our children's lives. We cannot control their genetic bents. We cannot control all of the influences that prey on them each day. The good news is that because we have a sovereign God (a God who wields ultimate control), we don't *need* to control these things. If we didn't have the security that the things and events beyond our control still fit within the overall plan of God, it would be very difficult to be courageous. The reason is obvious: Uncertainty is one of the primary causes of fear.

But faith looks at the uncertainties of life, our human inadequacies, and our inability to manipulate circumstances through the reality of a sovereign God. He promises that He is adequate for every situation He permits in our lives. From Romans 8:28 we learn He has promised to orchestrate every situation in our life for the good of those who are committed to Him.

I was speaking to a bunch of teenagers at a summer camp on the subject of maintaining moral purity in their dating lives. We had discussed how to avoid temptation and the importance of being willing to take a stand if pressured to compromise.

A girl came up to me afterward and told me about an evening she spent with a guy she had been dating for a few months. He supposedly shared her commitment to Christ as well as her high moral standards. But on this particular night as they drove through the countryside from her home to the town where they were to meet some friends, he suddenly pulled the car off the road and proceeded down a dirt path into the woods.

He didn't waste any time letting her know what he wanted. And she didn't waste any time telling him that not only was she *not* interested, but that their date and their dating relationship had come to an abrupt halt.

He wasn't inclined to take no for an answer and began to overpower her and tug at her clothing. Her parents had warned her about date rape and had given instructions on how to avoid situations where she could be attacked. Fortunately, her parents had also anticipated just such a scenario as developed that night and had given her a plan to cope with it. Her father had told her that sometimes she could take every precaution and a guy might still try something. If that ever happened, she had one other powerful weapon for protection. Her father's words shouted from her heart as her "boyfriend" tore at her clothes: "If you ever find yourself in a predicament like that, PRAY. Ask God to send His angels to pull that guy off of you."

Trembling with fear, she followed her father's advice. She used this horrible challenge as an opportunity to trust God. She pleaded to Him for help.

She had barely whispered her prayer for help when they heard a loud "thump" on the hood of the car. They both jumped. He immediately sat up straight behind the wheel. The quiet and darkness of the woods added to the fear in his heart. On the other hand, this girl said at that moment she became overwhelmed with calm. She knew full well that whatever it was that caused that sound on the hood came because of her prayer.

When he finally got up enough guts to open the door and look around, he saw that part of a tree limb had fallen across his hood.

He came back into the front seat and began again to push for her to surrender sexually to him, although this time he was only using words. She refused. That's when he said, "Either put out, or get out."

It took a lot of courage. But she calmly replied, "I'm not going to have sex with you."

At that point he reached across to the door

handle, threw the door open, and pushed her out into the woods. As quickly as he did that, he pulled the door shut, locked it, started the car, and turned it around.

She pleaded for him to let her in and take her home, but the roar of the engine and his determination to leave her behind drowned out her pleas. Because of the woods, he couldn't drive as fast as he wanted to, and she did her best to keep up with him. But his tail lights pulled further away from her even though she ran as fast as she could.

She saw his brake lights go on, then saw him take a right turn onto the road. The woods grew instantly silent and black. But she didn't feel alone. She felt God was with her and she kept going in the direction she last saw his tail lights.

Her house was several miles to the left of where they came in, so she crossed the highway and walked toward home. Again she prayed. "Thanks for saving me from him, Lord. I'm still frightened. Please get me safely home." Once again the prayer was barely spoken when she heard the sound of a car in the distance approaching from behind. It was headed in her direction but she didn't know whether to run for cover or just keep walking.

The choice was made for her by the speed of the car. It had her in its headlights before she could duck into the shadows. She kept walking. The car slowed down as it approached her and came to a stop a few hundred feet ahead. Then it started backing up. She held her breath. A woman's voice called out, "Can we offer you some help?" The voice sounded familiar. As the car finally pulled next to her, the people inside had turned on the interior lights so she could see them. It was her pastor and his wife returning from town. She thought she could almost see the angel opening the car door for her.

"What about the guy?" I asked.

That's when this girl simply smiled and said, "His car had engine trouble not far from where he had exited the woods. He ended up walking several miles to town. From my best calculations, he started his walk about the time a terrible thunderstorm struck."

God may be the only person willing to stand by us when we're forced to stand alone, but as this girl found out, one person and a sovereign God make a majority.

Real Power

Just before Jesus ascended to heaven He told His disciples it was essential that He leave, in order that the Spirit could come. This is the same Comforter that He had discussed with them before the crucifixion. He was the promised Power that they would receive after He left (Acts 1:8).

If we genuinely want to build courageous children we must show them the way to God. It doesn't happen through family devotions, church, Sunday school, or parochial education. These all have their place and play a part. But the primary responsibility falls on us as ambassadors of God's love, power, and grace. When it's real in us, they don't miss it.

Probably no other feature of the Christian gospel stands out so boldly as the sheer power of love that drove Jesus to the cross. And probably no other enigma of the Christian movement haunts us so much as the sheer lack of appropriation of that power in the Christian's life.

For those who seek, however, there is much to find. Those willing to take the Creator at His word, or a Savior on the grounds of His reputation, savor a sweet surprise. The God of Abraham, Isaac, Jacob; the God who helped David drop Goliath; the God who spared Shadrach, Meshach, and Abednigo the heat, or Daniel the teeth; the God who whispered in a virgin's ear and then multiplied in her womb—He is the Author of Courage.

He calls the rank and file to greatness, the obscure to notoriety, the weak to victory, the crippled and lonely to the finish line. With Him we're everything; without Him we don't have a prayer.

When our sons let God's power burn in their soul they develop the ability to resist scorn and the wisdom to draw near to people who share their common faith. When our daughters embrace an abiding confidence in God, their lives stand out, too. They prove that:

- You don't need to be glamorous to be pretty.
- You don't need influential friends to be significant.
- You don't need money to be wealthy.
- You don't need muscles to be strong.
- You don't need academic degrees to be wise.
- You don't need titles to have impact.
- You don't need to be tall to be looked up to.

Throughout this book, we've developed principles about courage. They mean little, however, without God. The power behind these principles comes from trusting in the Lord. Without Him these principles can only take you so far. Only when you place them in a heart that beats for God do you see what real courage is.

The truth is, on our best day, with our most gallant effort, we can stand only so long. Most of our enemies are bigger than us. We can do our apprenticeship, leverage our fears, and jump through all of the other hoops . . . but still fall flat.

Unless we remember who is ultimately in charge. We need to join our spirit with the God who is bigger than any of our problems and stronger than any of our challengers.

Power Behind the Tears

If you've studied the prophet Jeremiah, you know tears were never far from his cheeks. They gushed often as he watched a faithless nation turn its back on God. He also suffered the pain and isolation when they turned on him. But he didn't back down because he knew there is a God in heaven who empowers His children on earth. It was a truth he had known since childhood.

> Then the word of the LORD came unto me, saying, Before I formed thee in the belly I knew thee; and before thou camest forth out of the womb I sanctified thee, and I ordained thee a prophet unto the nations. Then said I, Ah, Lord GOD! behold, I cannot speak: for I am a child.

> But the LORD said unto me, Say not, I am a child: for thou shalt go to all that I shall send thee, and whatsoever I command thee thou shalt speak. Be not afraid of their faces: for I am with thee to deliver thee, saith the LORD (Jeremiah 1:4-8, KJV).

Do not be "afraid of their faces." A relationship with the Lord God through His Son gives us a strength nothing in the universe can conquer. The apostle Paul gropes for words to describe the overwhelming power we have in Christ:

> I pray that the eyes of your heart may be enlightened, so that you may know what is the hope of His calling, what are the riches of the glory of His inheritance in the saints, and what is the surpassing greatness of His power toward us who believe. These are in accordance with the working of the strength of His might which He brought about in Christ, when He raised Him from the dead, and seated Him at His right hand in the heavenly places (Ephesians 1:18-20).

God has placed in us the same power that surged in Christ when the Father raised Him from the dead. With that power He wants us to exercise courage. When we put our confidence in the God who's ultimately in charge, we demonstrate the source of our courage to our children.

Courage to Face Today

We need it right now, don't we? Even while you're reading this book you're thinking of some of the crosses you drag around, some of the Goliaths who hurl threats at your reputation, some of the lions that roar from the den you've been thrown into. God wants to empower you *now.*

You think of the challenges that face your children. You want to intervene, isolate their threats, and let their enemies have it. But that's a luxury you probably won't get to enjoy.

The good news is that God is with us. It's more than a cliché. It's a reality, it's true, and it's going to remain true whether we acknowledge it or not. If we want to appropriate His power, we must be willing to exercise faith. And that takes courage.

To be honest with you, I've come to a conclusion about courage that I expect the world to reject: The most courageous position we can assume is on our knees.

Those who understand this understand the sheer and infinite force behind God's promises. It enables them to trust Him for the things they can't see and to face the enemies that glare at them each day.

Courage to Face Tomorrow

God wants to give us courage to face the battles rumbling in the distance. We know they're there. Some would like to stay put, hold back, take no risks. But courageous people would rather make their bed in the narthex of hell before submitting to an empty life of timidity. Since the challenges that face us are part of God's plan for our good, we can enjoy them only by stepping out of our comfort zones.

Maybe you're facing the prospect of a new baby. Or maybe you're on the other side of the spectrum. Soon you're going to dust and polish an empty nest, and for the first time in your busy life you shudder at the prospect of a quiet home. Maybe the home-grown heroes you're trying to influence have visitation rights every other weekend. The future intimidates as you see it offering so little opportunity.

If today is a wilderness, then tomorrow is the promised land. Whatever we know about God, of this we can be certain: the God who has brought us this far is able to take us all the way. His track record is unblemished.

When you wander through Faith's Hall of Fame (in Hebrews 11), you realize how much power a sovereign God wields over the future. You see how He worked to secure the future of the men and women who put their confidence in Him: Abel, Enoch, Noah, Abraham, Sarah, Isaac, Jacob, Joseph, Moses, Rahab, Gideon, Barak, Samson, Jephthah, Samuel, David, Daniel. People . . .

> who by faith conquered kingdoms, performed acts of righteousness, obtained promises, shut the mouths of lions, quenched the power of fire, escaped the edge of the sword, from weakness were made strong, became mighty in war, put foreign armies to flight. Women received back their dead by resurrection; and others were tortured, . . . others experienced mockings and scourgings, yes, also chains and imprisonment. They were stoned, they were sawn in two, they were tempted, they were put to death with the sword; they went about in sheepskins . . . being destitute, afflicted, ill-treated (men of whom the world was not worthy). . . . And all these, having gained approval through their faith, did not receive what was promised, because God had provided *something better* . . . (Hebrews 11:33-40, emphasis mine).

These were the people who didn't let the

intimidations of the world stop them from doing what they knew was right. They heard the shouts of the crowd, but they stood firm to the promises of God.

The crowd still tries to outshout the courageous. They scream at the handfuls of moms and dads who want to make a difference.

"Put that kid in day care. For crying out loud! What are you, a dinosaur or something? You've got a brain that evolved for a reason, and the reason was not for it to waste away taking care of a home. Get a life, woman. Get a career!"

"You want to spend your Saturday with the kids? Are you nuts? Listen, I've got a 9:30 tee time and I expect your tail to be there with spikes on. This client is too important, and he wants to talk with *you*. I need you to help close the deal. Your kids will be home when you get back. Besides, it's Saturday. You've earned yourself some personal time."

"Why fight it? They're just going to jump in the back seat the first chance they get. Forget all of this scruples training. This is the twenty-first century! Give them the birth control of their preference and be done with it."

There aren't many brave left. I wonder if there ever were very many? One thing is certain: for those few who are willing to follow God over the next hill, He promises that each step will get them that much closer to the glorious kingdom reserved for a faithful few.

Courage to Face Yesterday

One of the greatest obstacles to a courageous life doesn't loom on the horizon nor does it lurk in the corner of our daily lives. It haunts us from the corridors of our past. It's the gray ghost of doubt, anger, and hurt that keeps us chained to the regrets of yesterday. We try and try, but it's so hard to pull ourselves from its shackles.

But God's got the key.

He wants to turn the tumbler in the locks that keep us fettered. He wants to bring us out of the dungeons and into the light.

But it's hard because it takes so much courage to forgive.

Maybe that's why most people would rather rearrange the chips on their shoulder than refuse to put them there in the first place.

Maybe that's why we keep taking sips from that cheap whiskey called Revenge. It numbs our conscience and blurs our vision for truth.

Maybe that's why its easier to be defensive. It allows us the luxury of slipping out the back door of responsibility.

Maybe that's why we have a bad habit of throwing fuel on the anger that burns deep in our gut. It warms our fragile egos—even while it consumes our souls.

Cowardice plays right into the hands of a family that wants to shortcut their way through relationships. But courage demands that we do what it takes to reconcile the past with the present, to keep the dynamics between family and friends healthy.

When it comes to family, we find out quickly whether we've got what it takes to be courageous. Every once in a while, our ability to forgive gets tested beyond its limits. The hurts stack up on top of each other. We have to catalog the insults, and our willingness to close the door on our rage gets too exhausted to budge.

That's when we need to catch a glimmer from above.

In 1860, a family ran out of patience with each other. It was a big household with a network of limbs in her family tree that twisted and stretched their way throughout the territories of a young nation. This family had a proud name and a proud legacy. Throughout the world it was both respected and envied. Everyone called her "America."

But this family had a feud. A big one. And the issues that it fought over were not the nickel and dime type. They were the very fundamentals that determine whether a family's ancestors have a prayer.

And so America went to war against herself. North faced South, Blue met Gray, brothers fought brothers, fathers killed sons.

For more than five years, the cannons exploded, men marched, rifles fired, flags fell, bayonets plunged, blood poured. Before it was over, America would bury over one and a half million of her sons. More Americans died in the Civil War—killing each other—than in all other U.S. wars put together.

Shiloh: 24,000 men fell in two days.

Gettysburg: 53,000 men fell in three days. (By contrast, 56,000 American men died in the entire Vietnam War.)

One skirmish at Gettysburg—Pickett's Charge—claimed the lives of an entire Confederate division in just a few hours.

This carnage was chronicled—every battle, every victory, every bitter defeat. It was reported by newsman, romanticized by songwriters, probed by poets, and captured by photographers. The conflict made household names out of Walt Whitman, Sarah Barton, Frederick Douglass, Mary Chestnut. Of the photographers, Matthew Brady was the most famous. All tallied, more than one million photographs were taken of the Civil War.

And then it ended.

As soon as it was over, the people of America wanted to forget it. They didn't want to read stories of the horrors of battle. They wanted new poems, new prose, new songs to hum. But most of all, they didn't want to see any more pictures. They wanted to move beyond their loss, to rebuild their hopes and see if they could dream again.

Matthew Brady declared bankruptcy. Photographers couldn't find newspapers or magazines willing to buy their pictures. They were left without a means to maintain a livelihood and grew desperate to recover anything they could of their capital investment.

Tens of thousands of their negatives had been exposed on panes of glass. That's how pictures were made on the battlefield. The horrors of war imprinted themselves on a sheet of glass at the rear of the camera. Once back at their makeshift darkroom, the men would print a positive image on photographic paper.

Some photographers found a buyer for their glass. Greenhouse builders were anxious to take such wares off their hands on the cheap, and massive glass houses were soon built with photographer's negatives.

And the images of the dreadful conflict lived on.

The men and women who worked in these

greenhouses couldn't escape the memories. Every day the ghosts of war stared back at them as they peered through the glass.

A father would lift his gaze from working over roses to fix his eyes on an image of a young soldier's twisted remains and grisly death mask on his face. It would remind him of the son he lost in Virginia. A wife's tears would spill over flower petals as she thought of a husband who didn't come back, buried in some forgotten field in Georgia. Every time she looked up, she would have to remember.

But day after day the sun shone through the glass images, and little by little they would fade. It took years for some of the darker images. But eventually, sunlight bleached all the painful memories to a faint silhouette.

Meanwhile, new life was growing from the soil inside the greenhouse. The sweet aroma of flowers replaced the stench of war.

God's forgiveness works like that.

Forgiveness isn't an event, it's a process based on an event, and sometimes the process takes time.

We're slipping through our schedule, doing our best to live courageously, when something glares at us from our memory. Without wanting to, we catch a dim glimpse of a painful regret etched on the window of our soul.

We want to stop. We want to quit. We want to surrender.

Courageous people don't.

They just lean a little closer to the Light of the World, warming their hearts with His grace, basking in the radiance of His love.

By and by, the images fade. Eventually, we have to squint to remember. Meanwhile, a divine fragrance drifts through our lives, sweetening the kinships closest to our heart.

The God of our past, our present, and our future is a God who blesses courageous homes.

He upholds us today.

He secures tomorrow.

And He gives us the power to reconcile with yesterday.

Such is the God who will enable you to pass these gifts to your own home-grown heroes.

Courage Is Contagious

July 2, 1863. A small rocky knoll outside a little village in central Pennsylvania called Gettysburg. It's a long story, leading up to a brief battle. I won't share the details—we'll let the Civil War historians do that. But I'll tell you two undisputable conclusions about what happened there. The courageous effort of the Twentieth Maine Regiment turned the battle of Gettysburg in the favor of the North. And the courageous actions of Colonel Joshua Chamberlain singularly kept his men from retreating from the superior forces of the Fifteenth Alabama Regiment.

It's one of the textbook cases that military leadership study today. Not so much because of what happened, or even how it happened, but *why* it happened. The Twentieth Maine should have been defeated—all things considered.

They were battle scarred. They had paid some hefty dues already. It was near Antietam Creek in western Maryland that they first heard the whistle of Confederate bullets around them (in September 1862). Whatever romantic notions these woodsmen, farmers, and fishermen from Maine had when they enlisted in the Union Army were quickly dashed by the sobering sights and sounds of war. Antietam was to be one of the bloodiest conflicts of the entire nightmare known as the Civil War. In December of 1862, they had fought in the battle of Fredericksburg. It was at Fredericksburg that they bivouacked all night among their dead. They were pinned down by the Confederates and couldn't move from their ghoulish surroundings. The images of those battles were still swirling in their heads as they marched toward their position.

They had hiked one hundred miles in five days. They were in the middle of a desperately needed nap when they were summoned to take position in the unguarded rocks called Little Round Top. It was there where they would shift the weights on the balance. It was there where they would begin the ending of the war. Three hundred and eighty-five men became overwhelmed with courage because of their deep-seated convictions about the union of states, and because of the standard set by their commanding officer.

Joshua Chamberlain had not been bred for the battlefield. But his upbringing had groomed him for greatness. He was a compassionate Christian man who had learned admirable character traits as a child. His father had instilled self-discipline, will, and perseverance. He was the son of farming parents in Maine. Farming Maine in the middle 1800s was a great place to learn character. Maine is that patch on the map where the earth continues to surface rocks from deep beneath its soil. The Chamberlains were used to dealing with this phenomenon in their fields. Joshua and his brother had been assigned the task of removing the rocks from a field that his father planned to plow. They returned one day to tell their father that they had encountered a particularly stubborn rock that was too large to move. He simply said, "Go move it." And so they did. This was one example of many where his father taught him that when a task looked impossible, that was the time to attack it.

As Colonel Chamberlain studied the scene from his vantage point on Little Round Top, he realized that the Union Army was in an extremely vulnerable position. Retreating or surrendering would have guaranteed him and his men their lives, but it would have forfeited the convictions that brought them to the battlefield in the first place.

When Chamberlain ordered his men to charge the Alabama Regiment it was easy for them to comply—because Chamberlain was leading the attack. Even though they were exhausted, hungry, and stinging from the heavy casualties they received in their initial skirmish with the Alabama Regiment, they rose up and charged into what appeared to be their certain death. They didn't have to be prodded or coerced. The example of their courageous colonel was all they needed. As they screamed their way into the Confederates, a Southern officer fired his pistol at

Chamberlain at point-blank range—and missed. He immediately handed his sword to Chamberlain who by this time had his own sword at the officer's throat.

Where does such uncommon courage come from? Joshua Chamberlain had learned daily courage at the knees of his parents. When, as a teenager, he decided to study the New Testament in its original language, he isolated himself in the attic during the winter months and studied from morning to night until he had mastered the intricacies of Greek grammar.

He spent three years in seminary preparing to be a minister. They didn't have to teach him the biblical ethics of respect, compassion, and selflessness. They were already deeply embedded in his character. It was his firmly held beliefs in the ideals of the union—freedom, justice, equality, and human dignity—that motivated him to sign up for duty in the Civil War. At the time he was a professor of languages at Bowdoin College, a husband, and a father. The college tried to persuade him not to enlist by offering him two years of travel in Europe. But he made his choices because of convictions, not conveniences.

As a result of his heroics at the Battle of Little Round Top, Joshua Chamberlain received the Medal of Honor. As you turn the pages of Civil War history, his record jumps out as one of the most remarkable. A total of fourteen horses were shot out from under him. He was wounded six times. At Petersburg, while leading his brigade in a charge against a superior Confederate fortification, he was wounded in both hips. For his bravery that day, he was promoted to brigadier general. It was the only time a man was promoted to that rank on the field of battle in the entire war.

His infectious courage changed the outcome of several battles. Five months after his horrible wounds to his hips, he left the hospital despite the doctor's desire and reported to the front even though he was barely able to walk or ride. He led his men from January 1865 through the surrender at Appomattox in April of that same year. Two crucial battles—Quaker Road and Five Forks—became Union victories because of his courageous leadership.

On March 29, during the battle of Quaker Road, Chamberlain was leading his brigade in an attack. A Confederate bullet passed through the large muscle in his horse's neck, hit a metal mirror in his shirt pocket, penetrated the skin, followed his ribs around to his back, and came out the other side of his coat. Both Chamberlain and his horse slumped over, bleeding heavily.

It is not certain how long he lost consciousness, but when he came to, he saw the right side of his attacking brigade retreating. With his coat soaking with blood, he spurred his bleeding horse to the center of the retreating men and ordered them to attack. When they saw their commander in bad need of attention, forsaking his own needs for the cause before them, they were filled with courage. They turned, attacked, and won the battle. It weighed heavily in the surrender of General Lee's forces the next month. For his "conspicuous gallantry," Chamberlain was promoted to major general.

Joshua Chamberlain is an excellent example of the affect that courage can have on people. Courage tends to multiply when it's in the right crowd. It's amazing how many people can be empowered by one person's resolve. That's why Joshua Chamberlain stands as a fitting example. It takes a lot of courage to fight against overwhelming odds.

It also takes a lot of courage to show grace when you have the advantage.

For his courageous leadership on the battlefield, General Grant selected Chamberlain to command the special honor division of veteran brigades formed for the surrendering of arms and colors of the Confederate Army at Appomattox. The Twentieth Maine was there. As General Joshua Chamberlain stood beside his men he wore the marks of a warrior, but inside his uniform beat the heart of a sensitive and compassionate man. As he looked upon the tattered remains of the once-great Confederate Army, he was overwhelmed by their defeated and dejected expressions. Even though he had once faced them on the battlefield, they were still his fellow countrymen. His Christian convictions ruled his life, and to the shock of the entire world, Chamberlain ordered his division to "present arms"—a token of respect reserved for someone in superior rank or position. It was a humbling gesture of human compassion that ignited the dying ember of pride and self-respect in the Confederate soldiers, and helped ease their humiliation in defeat.

Courageous teachers beget courageous students, courageous leaders beget courageous followers. Best of all, courageous parents beget courageous children.

There's a vital truth about courage that everybody needs to understand:

Courage is contagious.

We communicate more from our life than from our lips. If we want to infect the people around us with the real thing, then our lives need to reflect the very virtue we long for them to embrace.

This isn't easy.

You're Corporal Dad or Major Mom out in the trenches of life and there's lots of parents hanging around you. They're sitting next to you in the bleachers at the Little League game. The salvos of life have been beating them down. They want to give up. They're so whipped that they're thinking marriage isn't worth it, the hassles with their kids aren't worth it, the rat race isn't worth it. They'd rather surrender to distractions or indulgences, and in the process, surrender those vital years when their children so desperately need their help. We need parents out there who believe in the cause of family and are willing to pay the price. One mom or dad with courage can empower a bleacher full of defeated parents.

You're also surrounded by some significant individuals who look a lot like you. They have your hairline, your chin, or maybe that subtle way you shuffle when you walk. They have enough of a belief in the things that really matter to be willing to join you on the battle front. They have dreams waiting to be realized and internal gifts ready to be developed. But these same people are threatened by the discouragements that slip through the cracks of their fragile spirits. The bursts from culture's cannons explode around them. The temptation to run, to take the easy way out, or to surrender to their moral enemies is an enticing option. They turn to you for a cue.

At this point, they need your *example* more than they need a pep talk. If the convictions of your heart are great enough to lift you from the safety of the bunker to the smoke of the battlefield, then your children are more likely to follow. A nudge in the right direction could change the course of their lives.

And so it really comes down to you.

You're the Chamberlain in your children's lives.

You're their hope for confident, courageous living.

You're their assurance that the battle is worth fighting.

Throughout the pages of this book, I've done my best to develop and illustrate how to build courage into your children's hearts. I've outlined eight principles vital to a life characterized by courage. But they're merely concepts on a page—ideas and ideals that sound glorious—but make no difference—unless they're embedded and embodied in a willing heart.

The X factor in the equation is *you*. You determine whether courage will be a concept in your child's head or part of his "second nature."

You can't transfer something so precious from a textbook. You can write principles in the back pages of their Bible, put checklists on the refrigerator door, and wax eloquently around the dinner table. But if they don't smell the gunpowder on you, the rhetoric will be little more than empty nouns and verbs. Reality dictates that when it comes to courage, you can't rally the troops by photocopying some slogans and distributing them around the foxhole.

You must lead the charge.

Your children are *potentially* courageous, but potential turns into reality when love takes its stand. And though I've never met you, there's one thing I feel confident about you: you *do* love your children—probably more than you love yourself. As an honest adult, you are painfully aware of the challenges that wait to ambush them in the future. When they walk onto those distant battlefields, they won't have the luxury of deferring to you. They will be the field commanders of the new generation, and their best chance for victory is in your hands right now.

So give them a gift. Make these eight principles of courage *yours.* Lead from the front. Make your life an indisputable example of courageous living.

And watch what happens.

Behind the immature eyes, a young mind will be taking careful notes. From the midst of the confusion of childhood, a developing volition will draw confident conclusions. Within the magical world of a youthful heart, a spirit will be groomed for greatness.

And take comfort in the certainty that you won't be alone on that battlefield. There are a lot of parents who, like you, believe the cause is great enough, and the children worth enough, to pay the price for victory. Together, we can rally under the shadow of the cross, and watch our offspring enjoy the victories of courage for years to come.

There is one challenge that remains. And it's the one battle that we can't afford to lose.

When Courage
Hits Home

It was a full family function. We had built up this day for weeks. Each time we discussed it, Cody's heart swelled a little bigger with anticipation. This was one of his "rights of passage." After this day, he would no longer be a *little* boy.

No, this day, with all of its cuts, bruises, and tears, would entitle him for the next six years of his life to go by the moniker "boy" with all of the rights and privileges thereto.

He was awake before anyone else. He crawled in next to me and pushed his face into mine—less a need for affection than a need for attention. "Don't sleep, Dad, it's time to get up." I did, along with everyone else, to make the final preparations. This day was to be a rehearsal for life.

Cody was going to learn to ride without training wheels.

As I removed the training wheels from his bicycle, I thought of the time, over three and a half decades before, when my father had removed the training wheels from my bike. It had been a big family event for us, too, as my older brothers, younger sister, and my mother gathered around to watch me take my first ride. My best recollection was that it lasted about six seconds—cut short by a detour into the drainage ditch next to the road. I had planned a safer and softer location for Cody to endure his first lumps to freedom.

Darcy manned the video camera, Karis assumed the role of cheerleader, and Shiloh held down the blanket under the tree (preoccupied with chasing ants with her finger). Cody and I had taken up our positions on the sidewalk at the north end of the park. From there, the grass made a gentle slope down to a soccer field.

I stood behind him as he straddled his bicycle and we both surveyed the situation. My right hand was over his chest and I could feel his heart pounding. Anticipation and fear. At that moment it was primarily anticipation. But a few seconds into his solo ride, I knew that fear would be responsible for the bulk of his pulse rate.

A few final instructions, one more word of encouragement, a kiss on his left cheek, and he was off. To the applause and cheers of his family, Cody pedaled his way down the hill, past the goal posts, and crashed about twenty yards into the soccer field. He was up dancing around the bike before we got to him. We all enjoyed the celebration. He had survived his maiden ride on a two wheeler and we wanted to savor that moment.

But lest he confuse luck with success, we made him take several runs down the hill before we loaded his bike into the back of the car and returned home.

As Darcy and I watched his blond hair bob in sync with each rut in the terrain, we knew we were watching a metaphor. Within this little scene in the park, a son was not only a student, but a teacher. Our hearts took careful notes.

At first I ran alongside of him, encouraging, advising, and occasionally reaching out to grab the back of his seat to keep him from falling. But with each attempt, he grew more confident, with each recovery he became more daring, and with each success, he pedaled faster and further until eventually he left me bent over, huffing for air, watching him ride away.

He didn't ride far. Not that day. But he would, eventually. He had to. That's what he was made to do. He was never ours to keep, only to prepare for that day when his plans and purposes would take him over the hill and out of sight for good. It's a painful reality, but it has to happen. And it's good.

Oh, he'd be back. But not to stay. Only to visit. And that, too, was good. We could argue, like so many, that little would change when he finally left home, that the tight-knit family we enjoyed during his childhood would always stay intact. But we'd only be kidding ourselves. If we did anything to insure that things would stay the same, we would only kill the man in the boy. He was intended by God to move on, and only selfishness would want to keep that from happening. Today we were a resource; someday we would become a reference point.

For now, he was tethered to us. Three times each day we would reel him into the northeast chair at the family table, nourishing his body as well as his soul. He was still close enough to call out for help in getting down from a tree or for a solution to one of life's many riddles.

But the dependence that mark his early years will eventually yield to the independence of growing up. As he peddles further from our lives we will have to make a courageous choice to let him go. He'll master the two wheeler, but eventually he'll want to go back to four. Before very long he will be grabbing the car keys off of the hook in the kitchen and racing out the door.

Cody endured his first day without training wheels, just like he has endured so many other lessons in growing up. As we walked back to the car I held his bike in my left hand and Darcy's hand in my right. Her tight squeeze told me she had shared my thoughts. As we watched Cody and Karis up ahead, chattering about his success as a bike rider, we knew it was just a matter of time.

I don't worry much about him. He'll learn through his bumps and scrapes the lessons needed to survive. But at times I worry about me. It will be hard when he finally goes for good. It will be one of the hardest lessons I will have to endure. But it's a lesson I will have to take, and, for his sake, a lesson I will have to pass on.

Courageous love can't confine.

And the greatest lesson in courage we'll ever give them is when we exercise the courage to let them go.